T0129371

LIVING IN JOHN'S WORLD

Because He Can't Live in Mine

Patricia Sanderfer

 ARCHWAY
PUBLISHING

Scripture taken from The Holy Bible, New International Version®, NIV® Copyright © 1973, 1978, 1984, 2011 by Biblica, Inc.® Used by permission. All rights reserved worldwide.

Archway Publishing books may be ordered through booksellers or by contacting:

Archway Publishing
1663 Liberty Drive
Bloomington, IN 47403
www.archwaypublishing.com
1 (888) 242-5904

ISBN: 978-1-4808-7429-9 (sc)
ISBN: 978-1-4808-7428-2 (e)

Library of Congress Control Number: 2019900802

Print information available on the last page.

Archway Publishing rev. date: 2/5/2019

Dedicated to my loving husband, John,
whose strength and courage
carried him down the rocky journey of dementia.

CONTENTS

CHAPTER 1
Forbidden Fruit

I had just finished feeding him breakfast. I looked at his face, so strong and handsome. Tears were welling up in his beautiful brown eyes that still looked so intelligent.

"Is something wrong, John", I asked? There was no reply. He stared straight ahead with a far-off look as tears trickled down his face. I asked if he hurt somewhere or if he felt bad, but there was no response.

"Do you miss someone, John?" He glanced at me and nodded his head, yes. Each name I mentioned brought no response.

Finally, I said, "John, do you miss Pat?"

"Pat", he said, as his head dropped and his body shook with sobs.

I stood up and held him in my arms. "I am Pat, John, I am your Pat," I said, knowing that the words simply floated in the air and had not reached him at all. I wondered as I held him, at what place in our time together was the Pat he remembered and missed so much.

I can remember, as clearly as if it were yesterday, the first time I saw him even though that was more than thirty years ago. He came into the Civilian Club with another boy and stood on the edge of the dance floor. I was sitting with three girl friends in a half-circle booth next to where they were standing.

I was trying to watch the dancing, but my eyes kept going back to this handsome young man. His short military haircut could not keep the curly wisps of his black hair from giving him a tousled, windblown look. The lightweight jacket he wore did not hide the wide shoulders of his slender body. Too bad, I thought to myself. Even from here, I can see he is much too young for me to be interested in him.

My friends and I had talked about leaving the club to go home. I suggested that we ask the two young men if they would like to have our booth when we left.

Quickly, one of them slide into the booth beside one of my friends and John slide into the booth beside me.

They had just returned from Florida and their lively conversation convinced us that we didn't really have to leave so soon. They were air traffic controllers in the Air Force and they had been on temporary duty in Florida where they had worked in the tower during the lift-off of Apollo 11. They were still full of excitement from the great experience of participating in a space launch.

As he sat beside me his presence was so overwhelming that it was almost uncomfortable. His slightly up-tilted nose added a sort of impishness to his otherwise masculine face and beautiful, wide smile.

His tanned face was still slightly flushed from the sun and it seemed I could still smell the salt air. After getting a closer look, I realized I was right before. He was so young. Much too young for someone thirty years old, with an eight-year old child, to be feeling this attraction.

As the five of us sat talking, I felt his hand close over mine. I took his hand and laid it on the table. I said, "Look, Sonny, just because you saw The Graduate, doesn't mean I am Mrs. Robinson." We all laughed and I thought I had everything under control. As we started to leave, he asked if he could call me, but I told him I didn't think that would be a good idea.

A few days passed and I still could not get John out of my thoughts, but I felt I had made the right decision about the phone number. I had been married to a handsome man two years older than me and he spent most of the eight years we were married involved with other people. The last thing I needed was to get involved with a younger man.

When the phone rang, I was surprised to find that it was John on the line. "How did you get my number?" I asked?

He said, "You are the third person with your name in the telephone book so it didn't take long to get to you,"

I was amazed at the excitement I felt and my resolve to not see him melted away as we talked. My thought was that we could be friends. I wanted to keep him in my life somehow.

When he walked it was like poetry in motion. He seemed to walk on the balls of his feet, and he was as graceful as a large cat.

His shoulders were very strong, probably because playing baseball was his first love and all he ever wanted to do. Maybe he was a great baseball player because his arms and shoulders were so strong and his body was perfectly balanced with broad shoulders that tapered down to narrow hips. He was almost six feet tall with long arms and legs. So handsome, he was, with a smile that would melt the snow.

He thought he had a future in baseball and was being considered for a baseball scholarship, but the draft for the Vietnam War was imminent. If he was going to the war, he wanted to be in the Air Force so he enlisted. I was so glad, because it was the Air Force that brought him to me.

When he looked at me and spoke to me, he made me feel warm inside and somehow more special than I had felt in a long time or maybe never before.

I had to get ahold of myself. John had told me he was twenty-two years old. I had a brother that age. I certainly would not want my brother getting involved with an older woman; especially not with someone who was divorced and had a child.

Not trusting my emotions, I decided to take him to the Girl Scout camp and introduce him to my daughter. Once he sees her, I thought, the reality will hit him and he will pull away from the relationship on his own.

John was all for the visit to the Girl Scout camp. He brought my daughter a can of bug-off spray. Since he had spent most of his life in the woods hunting and fishing, he thought this would be the perfect gift. As it turned out, she was delighted to get it. The visit went well. Her presence in my life didn't seem to matter to him at all.

As the days passed and we spent more and more time together, I knew I was falling in love with him and I had to do something. It wouldn't work to tell him I didn't want to see him again, because I knew he would charm me out of that.

I knew a pretty young college student who was attending a college nearby. My plan was to invite her to dinner one night when John was going to be there and I was sure they would be attracted to each other.

The evening went just as I planned. We had a good time. They seemed to like each other and we laughed and talked. After a while she said she needed to get back to the college and left.

After the door closed, John turned to me and said, "You may not want me, but I can find my own girlfriends." After that, he turned and left my home.

It was hard to sleep that night, but pain was not a stranger to me. I had been hurt in my marriage and never wanted to experience loving someone and losing them again. I did not have the self-confidence to think I could hold on to this young, handsome man.

The days went by and I did not hear from John. Each time the phone rang, my heart would jump. I was afraid it was him and afraid it was not him.

One night, about one o'clock in the morning, the phone rang and it was John. John was an air traffic controller in the Air Force and the Communications Squadron. The group he was assigned to was on field exercises somewhere nearby. They were living and operating out of tents. John had waited until everyone was asleep and slipped back to the tent where the telephones were set up to call me.

We talked for a long time. Among other things, we talked about our age difference. The age difference did not matter to him and he convinced me that we would have a great time together.

CHAPTER 2
Friends or Lovers

The next few weeks were the most fun I had ever had in my life. John had an older model blue convertible car. My youngest brother was attending the junior college at Panama City, Florida. He lived in a small concrete block house on Thomas Drive across the street from the ocean.

I have since looked to see if I could tell where that house was, but Thomas Drive is now a thriving well-developed area of Panama City.

John and I, his friend, Bob, and Bob's friend, Ruby, would go to Panama City in John's old blue convertible and stay with my brother on the beach. We spent wonderful, fun-filled days in the sun and took long walks in the moonlight on the beach.

My brother was working as a bouncer at a local beach club to help pay his college expenses. The first night we went to the club, we went in and sat down at a table and ordered drinks.

The owner of the club came over and said to my brother, "Ed, I don't care if she is your little sister, we can't serve drinks to minors." We all thought this was funny because I was nine years older than anyone at our table.

My brother's small house was pretty full with him, his roommate and all of us. My brother didn't sleep much. He often strolled around the house to make sure that everyone was sleeping where they should be. I guess I shouldn't have been surprised that, after graduating from college in Washington, D.C., he became a secret service agent. No wrong-doings going on during his watch.

My brother had a German Shepard dog that he named, Pat, after me. Until this day, I wonder if that was a compliment or not.

I loved my brother. We had been close to each other all of our lives.

My brother met his wife during Spring break. After having been raised in Washington, D.C., she was a school teacher in Tennessee. She and some friends had rented a cottage very close to the little house my brother and his roommate were renting. She was tall like my brother with short blonde hair and a great figure. Her bubbly personality was contagious. I was glad he had met her.

At the end of the weekends, tired and happy, we would all head back to our homes in Georgia. John and Bob back to their jobs in the Air Force and I would go back to work at the Forestry Center where I was a secretary. I can't remember exactly what Ruby did. None of us had much money, but we could not have had more fun.

Toward the end of summer, John took a week's leave from the Air Force to visit his family in New York State. Every night he called and we talked for a while. Toward the end of the week, John said, "Someone wants to talk to you."

John's mother took the phone. I remember that I was standing by the bed and my knees went weak. I was afraid she was going to talk to me about John's and my age difference.

I sat down on the bed and talked to his mother. She said that since she was paying for the phone calls every day, she thought she should be able to talk to me. She was very pleasant and the conversation went well.

Very soon after John returned to Georgia, he told me that he and his friend, Bob, were being sent on temporary duty to Tennessee. The tour was for 90 days, but it was so hard to give him up so soon after we had met and 90 days seemed like a very long time. I wondered if his mother had called his commanding officer and convinced him that we should be separated for a while. If she did, neither John nor I ever knew this to be true.

After the end of the first 90-day tour, he was home for a while and then sent back to Tennessee for another 90 days. We wrote letters and I still have some of those. We talked on the telephone as much as we could.

Telephone calls were expensive. You were charged by the minute. We got together when we could and those times were precious.

John's tour of duty with the Air Force ended. He left to go back to his home in New York state. This put a large distance between us. John said he would be back as soon as he could get a job in Georgia. I wanted to believe him, but he was so young and I was afraid that once he got back to where he grew up with family and friends, he would not come back.

I missed him terribly, but life with my daughter went on and eventually I started dating. This time I dated men closer to my age. I used this time to remind myself that a future with John would not be good and tried to put this out of my mind.

CHAPTER 3
The Flame Subdued

One day, almost a year later, I got a call from John saying he was coming back. He said he had gotten a job as an air traffic controller at the local civilian airport.

I felt so many emotions; excitement to see him and apprehension about what this might mean. Did we need to pick up where we left off in a relationship destined to go nowhere? What about the man I was dating?

Time has a way of taking care of things. Getting back together was great. The fire was still there, but the flame had been subdued.

It was a fabulous new life for John. He loved his new job and the people he was working with. He was making more money than he probably ever imagined he would make. I was so proud of him. He moved into an apartment with a couple of other young men and they were having a great time. We went out together pretty often and occasionally I would go to a party at his apartment or just visit him there. He was living the life I envisioned for him.

We were close in that we had to talk or see each other pretty often. It was like we had to reassure each other that we were still there for each other. We didn't have a commitment or an agreement. Back then a commitment was "going steady". I felt sure he was dating other girls and I kept seeing my friend. I didn't have a commitment with him either.

Time went on and life was fun. My John was close by and I could reach out and touch him when I needed to. After all, it was the seventies.

Eventually, a friend of mine told me that John had been dating a girl that she worked with. I knew the girl and knew she was also dating a man from another town. She was pretty and nice so far as I knew. I didn't have a problem with it. After all, that is how it was back then, unless you were going steady. Also, you didn't have sex when you were going on casual dates or most of us didn't. It was certainly not expected.

One night I got a call from John. He asked me if I could come to his apartment. He said he needed to talk to me and he couldn't do it in front of my daughter. Of course, I immediately went to see him. As soon as I walked in the door, I knew something was very wrong.

He fixed us a drink and we sat down on the couch. He said that he had been seeing someone pretty often. I told him that I knew that, had known it for a while and that I knew her. Then he blurted it out, she was pregnant and she had told him that it was his baby.

This hit like a ton of bricks. This have your cake and eat it, too, life we had been living had just tumbled down. I asked him if he thought it was his and he said it could be. He asked me if I knew if she was seeing anyone else. I didn't answer right away and all of these thoughts went through my mind.

If I told him that I knew that she sometimes dated this other guy, he would not marry her. What if it was his baby? This would be a terrible mistake and the baby would pay the price. Having a baby out of wedlock in the seventies was not a small thing for the mother or the baby. If it was his baby, this was pretty remarkable. He was going to be a father.

I told him I didn't know whether she was dating anyone else or not. It was the right thing to do. I knew he would do what was right because that was the kind of person he was. It wasn't like it was someone he hardly knew. They had been seeing each other for a while.

I stayed most of the night and the pillows were wet with tears as we lay there and just held on to each other. It was over between us forever. Had we made the right decisions along the way. We didn't know and now it didn't matter. I eased out of the door after he finally went to sleep and I didn't talk to him for many years after that.

I don't know how I made it home. Although I had always thought of John as "forbidden fruit", there was a bond between us and it was hard to believe that it was broken. I felt empty inside. Part of me was missing. Had we been careless with something that was precious? Now it was too late.

Five years went by with no communication. I presumed they had married and that the child was born. I didn't want to know the details.

One day I got a call from John. He was getting a divorce. I was not surprised that the marriage had not worked. He told me he had a little girl and talked about how much he loved her. He had no doubts that she was his daughter. It had been a good decision to not tell him what I knew.

He told me he had hired a lawyer and when I asked him who he had hired, I knew it was not a good choice, but it was done. She had hired one of the best lawyers for women in town, a real womanizer, and it turned out to be a terrible experience for John.

I wondered if he lost so much because he was the one who filed for the divorce or because he was that boy from New York who came South and got this pretty little Southern girl in trouble and now wanted to leave her. That was how things were in the seventies. It left him pretty bitter. She had accused him of things he said he did not do.

John and I did not start back dating. I was dating a man six years older than I and was very happy in this relationship. He was the Base Commander of the Air Force Base nearby. We had a lot of friends and went to a lot of parties and military functions. This was a committed relationship. This relationship ended when the Commander retired from the Air Force and moved to Texas where he grew up. I didn't want to follow him there.

From time to time I talked to John and occasionally saw him through the years. It seemed our time had passed, but we still needed to stay in touch.

In 1993 I saw him in a restaurant. We kept glancing at each other. He was by himself and I was with several friends. After a while, I went over to where he was sitting and asked if he knew who I was.

"Of course," he said. It was not the leap of joy I had sometimes imagined it would be, but a lot of time had passed since we last saw each other. He had married again and gotten divorced. I knew he had married, but I didn't know he was divorced again. He asked if he could call me and I said, "yes."

A few days later, John called and asked me to come to his home for dinner. I was pretty excited to be going to spend time with my dear friend of many years. It's going to be awkward at first, I thought.

When I drove into his driveway, I wondered if this was going to be a problem. John was a very proud man and his home was very modest although located on beautifully wooded land. I lived in a large two-storied home on a lovely street. None of this mattered to me and I hoped it would not to him.

He met me on the porch with a big hug and kiss. It felt so good and it felt so right. He had cooked dinner and it was delicious. He was an excellent cook and loved to do it. We had so much to catch up on. We talked so much that it was a wonder we ever finished eating.

John had lost his job as an air traffic controller when President Reagan fired all of them for striking. That was in the late seventies. Now, some lawyer thought she could get their jobs back for them and he was very excited about that. It was all he had ever wanted to do after he had left the Air Force and never got over being fired.

We dated for close to a year. During that time there was a huge ice storm. Most of the homes were without power and I lost power to my home. We weren't prepared for snow and ice since this was rare in our part of the state. Only people with four-wheel drive vehicles could travel and they were cautioned to stay home.

I had gas logs in the living room, but the house was cold and my stove was electric. Most of all it was dark and scary. There were no house lights, no street lights; just candles, a flash light and light from the fire.

I was so relieved to hear John's voice on the phone. He called to see if I was alright and I told him what was going on. He told me that he would be there in about thirty minutes. I was so afraid for him to come, but he had the right kind of vehicle and he had grown up driving in snow and ice.

What went from a disaster turned into a couple of days that I will always remember. We had so much fun. We put blankets and pillows in front of the fire to stay warm. John cooked on my charcoal grill. We had water, even hot water because the water heater was powered by gas. I really didn't care if the ice ever melted.

It wasn't all a perfect reunion. John was obsessed with getting his job back. The time kept dragging on with no chance of getting his job back. It was frustrating and disappointing for him.

We were older now and had gone through some trying times. We were no longer a couple of young people with stars in our eyes. We enjoyed our time together. It was comfortable and loving.

He spent a lot of time at a hunting camp with his buddies and often he seemed preoccupied. We never had a cross word or anything close to a disagreement, but, somehow, we drifted apart and finally stopped calling each other.

I didn't know he had suffered a heart attack followed by open heart surgery. If only I had known. Maybe if I had been with him, his recovery would have been better. This was in 1994.

CHAPTER 4
Together Again

It was New Year's Eve 2000. Several of my friends and I had each prepared a special food and we all got together to share it for dinner. We were all single, but none of us were dating each other. We were very good friends and this seemed like the perfect way to enter into the new millennium.

During dinner we talked about fun things in our past and wondered about the future. More than our future, we wondered about the future of our country. When you are in your fifties and sixties, you have lived through many changes, both good and not so good.

Our friend, Ron, who could really get on the band wagon when he expressed his concerns, talked about the fact that the privilege of all veterans being entitled to a military funeral was being taken away by the current administration. He said that he was proud of having served his country and he wanted a military funeral.

He also told us that he was getting his pilot's license during the next weekend. Ron had been an air traffic controller and this had always been his dream.

We were so proud for him, but the next weekend Ron was killed in a plane crash. He was not flying the plane; he was riding with a friend. The plane crashed and burned.

This was very hard for all of us who knew him. He was such a great guy, very smart and he treated his elderly father in a way that we all admired very much.

Ron and I had often talked about his friendship with my friend,

John, when they had worked as air traffic controllers together at the local airport. He liked John and understood why I had kept him in my heart all of these years.

If he saw John or heard anything about him from someone else, he always told me. He had not heard about John's heart attack. I am sure he would have told me if he had known.

Because the plane Ron was in burned, the names of the occupants were not put in the paper until positive identification could be made. Of course, we all knew he was dead and I wanted John to know.

I had not seen John for six years, but I called the phone number I had for him then. The phone had been disconnected. I located his daughter, Melody, and asked about her father. She said her Dad was very sick and living with his mother. She was very worried about his illness and distraught that he didn't have any health insurance. She said she thought he had Alzheimer Disease. She gave me John's mother's phone number.

John's mother answered the phone. I told her who I was and asked to speak to John. When he answered the phone, he seemed very happy to hear from me. I told him about Ron's death. He was shocked and saddened at the news. We talked about Ron for a while and then I asked John how he was doing. He said he was fine; that was John, always just fine.

I told him that he had been the love of my life.

He answered, "I still love you. Can we start over?" My heart leaped with joy, but sunk with sadness. I knew that for him there would not be much starting over. He had been diagnosed with Alzheimer disease or Vascular dementia.

When I found out when the funeral for Ron was going to be held, I called John and told him I would be glad to take him and his mother to the funeral. John told me he would like to go with me and asked me to discuss it with his mother.

His mother said she didn't think they should go to the funeral, but would like to go to the funeral home when the family would be receiving guests. We agreed upon a time and I told her that I would take them to the funeral home.

John's mother lived in a high-rise apartment building with controlled entry. I pulled up in front of the building at the time we had agreed upon. I got out of the car and stood beside it while I waited for them. My heart was pounding at the thought of seeing John after six years had gone by. He had sounded the same on the phone; would he be the same?

The door opened and John bounded out of the front door and hurried toward me with his arms open. He wrapped his arms around me and pulled me close to him. He had on a heavy sweater, but I could tell he was terribly thin. I buried my face in his sweater and a feeling of belonging came over me that had been missing for a long time.

As we drove to the funeral home, his mother was friendly and chatty. John did not have much to say, but he kept looking at me and smiling. I knew he was feeling what I was feeling.

We entered the funeral home. There was no body to view, but we greeted Ron's family and told them how sorry we were for their loss. Many of the friends that I shared with Ron were there and then I realized there was another group of people there.

Many of the air traffic controllers who had worked with Ron and John were there with their wives. It had been a long time since they had seen John and they gathered around him, hugging him and showing how fond they were of him. They didn't know he had been sick, but I could tell that they knew something was wrong.

They were seeing what I became aware of when we entered the bright light of the funeral home. John was so thin that the skin was pulled tightly on his face. His teeth were very prominent. My handsome John was indeed very sick. Still, he seemed to recognize everyone and they were sharing memories with him. I don't know if he remembered, but he was bluffing his way through pretty good. Several times, I heard him say, "Well, you know, it has been a long time."

After a while, John's first wife entered the room. She walked up to John and spoke to him. He spoke, but there was no sign of recognition in his eyes. She said, "Don't you remember me?" He said, "No, I am sorry, but I don't". This seemed to really please the air traffic controllers, especially their wives.

I figured they had formed their opinion during the very unpleasant divorce John had experienced during the time when they were working with him. As they say in the South, John got the short end of the stick.

When I took John and his mother to their home, John asked if he could call me. I gave him my phone number and told him that I would love to hear from him.

Later, when his mother was alone, she called me to tell me how sick he was. She told he that his memory was badly affected and that he could neither read nor write. I got the impression she didn't expect him to live very long. She said he had been diagnosed with Alzheimer disease two years ago, but he had continued to work and live alone until two months ago when he came to live with her.

He had not been able to find his way home from work one evening. He made it to the town where he lived, but could not remember how to get to his home. He stopped at the post office and asked them how to get to his home.

This is so indicative of this terrible disease. His memory failed him, but his mind told him that the post office would have his address and could tell him how to get home. The post office personnel notified the local authorities that he seemed to have a problem and they determined that they needed to notify his family.

In his mother's voice and words, I heard many emotions. She was hurt and angry that this had happened to him. He had always been there for her when she needed him and now, he was no longer able to care for her. She was dismayed and annoyed with his inability to perform many simple tasks.

She complained that he changed clothes too many times in a day and that he cut himself when he shaved and got blood on her towels. She said she wasn't able to take care of him. She was in her seventies.

I will help her take care of him, I thought to myself. I will spend time with him and make his last few months as comfortable and happy as possible. I didn't know much about the disease and had no concept of what this meant.

Patricia Sanderfer

CHAPTER 5
Our Journey Begins

I knew that John loved to be outdoors. He had hunted and fished all of his life. There was a large lake that had a public park pretty close to where John and his mother lived. For our first outing, I thought that the park would be a good place to go. It was January, but the weather was nice. John wore the same heavy sweater that he had worn to the funeral. The sweater concealed some of the thinness, but it was still visible in his face.

There was a sandy beach in the park. We held hands and walked along the beach. I remembered years ago when we had walked on the beach in Panama City. That had been over thirty years ago. I felt the same way when he took my hand as I did then. Well, it was almost the same.

The feeling of excitement I felt was diminished by the feeling of sadness that he was going to die soon. I was not getting a clear feeling of what he knew and didn't know. I knew he could not or should not drive, but I didn't know what else he knew or understood.

Somehow, I didn't want to take him to my house. The chemistry between us had always been so overwhelming. What would I do if he wanted us to be more than friends? We had been so much more than friends in the years past, but if I allowed this to happen again, it didn't seem right.

I didn't know if he was capable of making responsible decisions. If I turned him away, I was afraid it would hurt him. I didn't want to turn him away, I wanted to put my arms around him and tell him he was going to be alright. So, after our afternoon on the beach, I took him back to his mother's home.

On our next date, we went to dinner. From what his mother had told me, I didn't think he would be able to read the menu. I asked him what he wanted and he said he would have whatever I was having. I suggested several things and he indicated that chicken sounded good. I ordered for both of us.

That was the beginning of many experiences where waiters and waitresses looked at me like I was being rude or inconsiderate by ordering for us without giving him a chance to do it. I never got used to that.

Looking back, I wish I had printed some small cards that said he had dementia and might not be able to answer questions about his order. I didn't want to say anything in front of him.

We didn't talk much during dinner so I would smile every time he looked at me. I felt he would understand a smile better than anything. I watched closely what he was doing to see if he needed help with anything.

After noticing me watching him, he offered me some of his food. I guess he thought that was why I kept watching his plate. After that, I tried to be less obvious. He could actually feed himself very well. After dinner, I took him home to his mother's home again.

John called me every night. His mother told me later that he had written my phone number in many different places around the house. He was afraid he would lose it. He wouldn't talk very long, but we would talk about when we could get together again. He always told me that he loved me and I would respond that I loved him, too.

I can't keep putting this off, I thought. On our next date, I invited him to dinner at my house. I showed him the pole he had put up several years ago for me to hang a bird feeder on. He didn't say if he remembered or not, he just said that he was surprised that it was still there.

He was really good…a master of cover up. I asked him if he remembered coming to my house during an ice storm so that I wouldn't have to stay by myself. The electricity was off so we had no heat except for the gas logs in the fireplace. We had made a pallet on the floor in front of the fireplace and I really didn't care if the electricity ever came back on again. He said he remembered, but I was not sure that he did.

We ate dinner and then started to clear the dishes away. As we stood in the kitchen, he took me in his arms and kissed me on the lips. Then he said, "Wow, it has been so long since I kissed a woman." I knew then that he had been by himself for a long time.

The dishes didn't get done that night. We just sat and held each other until it was time for me to take him home. The years melted away and I knew I had him back for better or worse. I had no idea how "worse" it could get.

Eventually, I would pick John up on Friday night from his mother's home and take him home on Sunday night. He would bring clothes for the weekend. They were clean, but were pretty worn.

We started shopping for new clothes for him. It was so much fun and sometimes challenging. I didn't know much about men's clothing and what size he would wear, but we figured it out.

Pants had to be tried on to get the right size. When he would go into a dressing room, I couldn't go with him. I would pray that he could do it by himself and not come out with no clothes on or something like that. He did very well although it took a while and then he would come out and show me how they fit.

It was so much fun because he was so handsome in the clothes we bought. He could have been a male model. By February the clothing stores were putting their clothes on sale and we found a fairly high-end store that really cut their prices when they had a sale. We found some beautiful clothes and I could tell that he was proud of how he looked. He thanked me over and over.

Each Sunday night, he would change back into the clothes he came with and I would keep the new clothes at my house.

As we went from place to place, he always opened the door for me. When there were double doors, I wondered if he could read the words on the door or if it was just an automatic thing his mind did.

I finally figured out that he could read. We were riding down a four-lane road when we came to a traffic light. The light had turned yellow and I stopped. I commented that I was glad I stopped because there was a police car behind me in the other lane.

He looked over his shoulder and told me that it wasn't a police car, that it had a Forestry sign on the door.

Finding out he could read was an interesting discovery. When we were at home, I decided to find out how well he could read since his Mother had said he could not read. He could read all of the words in a line, but could not follow the words to the next line. That was useful information to know.

Each day brought new discoveries. John smoked and I worried about that. I didn't like the smell of tobacco in a house or car especially when it became old. I asked him if he would go out on the screened porch to smoke. He reached into his pocket, took out the package of cigarettes and handed them to me. He said, "I don't need those. Throw them away." I said, "Oh no, I am not asking you to quit smoking, just not in the house."

He insisted that he didn't want to smoke anymore so I told him that I would put them in the cabinet in the event he changed his mind. He never smoked again when he was with me and never mentioned it.

At first, John's mother, seemed to be okay with our seeing each other. She would call me and talk to me about John's life during the years we were apart. She had so much bitterness in her heart about the two women John had been married to. She went on and on about how terrible they had treated him. After hours of this, I began to feel sure that, in time, she would feel the same way about me.

During the time she talked about John's daughter's mother, she would make remarks about his daughter, too. She said that his daughter didn't care about him and gave some examples. This surprised me because I knew that John loved his daughter very much.

My first thought was to see if I could get the two of them back together. He needed his daughter now more than ever.

Even though she was studying to be a nurse, his daughter had not understood what was going on with her Dad. What she saw was a man who was losing a grip on life. He was not taking care of himself or his home and some of her attempts to reach out to him came up short.

She was also very busy studying and had married shortly after John had a heart attack and open-heart surgery. She knew something was wrong, but did not know he was developing vascular dementia and later was diagnosed with Alzheimer disease.

My heart still hurts when I think of him living alone during the time when his abilities to take care of himself were slowing slipping away. How frightening this must have been and how lonely he must have been. I wish I had known that he was sick and could have been there to help him through this time.

If I had been there and he had not been diagnosed at that time, it could have been tragic if I had not understood his behavior. I have observed that the behavior associated with this disease is often considered disgusting. That is a hard word, but when people can't perform simple tasks or act in ways generally considered appropriate, this is often the reaction.

His friends had disassociated themselves from him when his behavior began to change. If they had understood, I am sure that would not have happened. So maybe it was meant to be that we got back together when we knew why he was like he was.

John sold his convenience store the year he had a heart attack. He went to work as a store manager for a chain grocery store. By going through his files later on, I could see where his ability to work was diminishing. He was reassigned to a night-time manager and later to stock manager.

When he finally quit his job, he was a person who stocked the shelves of the store. I am sure the friends he had made along the way at the store were helping him perform his duties.

I began to make an attempt to rebuild the relationship with John and his daughter. This was easy to do because they had so much history.

He had taught her to hunt and fish and they had spent many hours together enjoying nature. I could see so much of John in his daughter. She was a kind, loving person with his easy-going nature.

As my relationship with John's daughter grew, my relationship with his mother diminished.

CHAPTER 6
New York State

"We are going to New York," John said. I asked if he meant the part of New York where he was born and had lived?

He answered, "Yes."

"When are you going, John?" He said he wasn't sure exactly when they were going, but it was going to be pretty soon.

"I am paying for everybody's ticket," John said. I asked how he knew that. He said he had heard his mother talking about it. He seemed to be upset about that.

Who is going with you, I asked. "My mother, my sister, Rachel, and all of her family. That is going to cost a lot of money. I don't know how much money I have or if I will have any left," he said.

I asked him what money he was talking about. He said his mother had sold his home and that she had his money, but he didn't know how much they sold it for.

I asked him if he had wanted her to sell his home and he said, "No, never. I had just finished paying for it and I loved my home. I could stand in my front door and watch the wild turkeys feeding in the woods and the deer that came up regularly. I had bird feeders behind my home and I loved watching the birds. I had a problem keeping the squirrels out of the feeders, but I liked them, too."

"My boats," he said. "Both of my boats were there and the shed where I kept my fishing stuff. Where are my things?" I told him I did not know, but that we would find out where they were.

His property was densely populated with big oak trees and some evergreens. He could have watched the oak trees waking up in the Springtime and the leaves turning from a soft green to a deep green as they matured.

In the fall, the leaves would turn from gold to orange and then to brown before they fell upon the ground. Fall was his favorite time of the year. The property was on a gentle sloping hill so he could see everything from his front door. It was a modest home, but there is a great feeling from being master of your own domain and he loved it.

I knew about the turkeys and the deer, because he had told me about them before and I had seen pictures. I had also seen the bird feeders when I was at this home. He had placed a metal shield on the wire to keep the squirrels out, but it didn't work very well.

The tears kept flowing down his face as he talked about it. I tried to comfort him, but I didn't know what to say. I knew he could not live there by himself and I guessed they needed the money to care for him, but he would not understand that.

I put my arms around him, wiped away the tears and went to the kitchen and got a Coca Cola for each of us. This was our favorite drink.

For a while, we sat on the porch and held hands until he was calm. Then we talked of other things to change the subject.

I told John's daughter, Melody, about his mother selling his property. She did not know this and just could not believe she would do this without telling her.

Later, his daughter and I went to the county where his property was located and looked at the papers concerning the sale of the property.

His daughter wondered if she was still the beneficiary of his life insurance policy for $50,000. John had always told her that she was the beneficiary, but she wondered if someone changed that, too? We decided to take John to see his insurance agent since he did not know if it had been changed or not.

The insurance agent had been a good friend of John's and this was a very good thing because he had added a clause to the policy that would make the payments on the policy if he was unable to work.

We arrived at the agent's office. He was glad to see John, but seemed reserved to meet his daughter and me. He had been talking to John's mother and she had made him believe that John's daughter did not care about him or his well-being. John asked him about the policy and he said that his sister, Rachel, was now the beneficiary and that John had agreed to that.

John told him that his daughter was supposed to be the beneficiary so the beneficiary was changed back to his daughter. After that, the agent gave John a big lecture about his having Alzheimer Disease and that the person who was going to be taking care of him should be the beneficiary. I am sure his intentions were good, but this really upset John.

Even after we returned home, he was hurt by the insurance agent's words. He had either forgotten that he had dementia or he did not like that the agent talked about it.

His daughter and I never mentioned the disease to him. We knew that he had been told by doctors and reminded by his mother so there was no reason to keep bringing it up. It served no purpose. We accepted his actions as the best he could do, because they were his new normal.

It was easy to redirect him away from something that would harm him by acknowledging what he wanted, why he wanted it and then asking if we could talk about it later. He needed validation that he controlled his destiny. He had been a strong, intelligent man who was kind and thoughtful of other people. He deserved that.

I don't believe that his mother had any idea how much he knew and how much he could understand because his memory was deficient in other areas.

This is a common mistake people make when dealing with a person with dementia. Not all of their mind is necessarily affected by the disease.

That is why we should always treat people with dementia as normal as possible and most certainly with respect. They feel, they hurt, they love just like they always did. The short-term memory is impaired, but what they are feeling in the present is very real.

He kept talking about the trip to New York. He had been born in a small town in the Southwest part of New York state.

I asked, "John, do you want to go?"

"Yes," he said, "but I don't want to leave you."

I said, "it will be so great for you, John. You haven't been there in a long time and you need to see your family. You are going to have so much fun. Why don't we just think about that part. I will be here when you get back and we can talk on the telephone while you are gone. Be sure and take my number with you."

Not wanting him to charge calls to me on someone's phone, I bought him a phone card with a hundred minutes on it. I knew he wouldn't be able to dial all of the numbers required to use it, but I told him to ask someone to help him. It never crossed my mind that anyone would not want him to talk to me. When I did not hear from him, I thought that might be what was happening.

John's daughter offered to set up a three-way call so that I could talk to him. She called and asked to speak to her Dad so they put him on the line. It was wonderful to talk to him and this was when I found out that he no longer had the phone card.

John and his family were supposed to get back home on Saturday. I didn't hear from him on Saturday night and I, of course, did not call him.

Sunday morning, I got a call from him and he began by saying, "Are you coming to take me to church?" I said that I would and then in the background I heard his mother ask who he was talking to. He told her he was talking to me and I could hear her very angry reaction.

In a soft voice he asked me to come on to get him and when she went in the bathroom, he would slip out of the door. I didn't want it to be this way, but I didn't think it was fair for him to be kept against his will.

I left as soon as I could and drove the 20 minutes to the parking lot of his building. He could see the parking lot from his window or maybe he was waiting at the door to the building. After a short time, I saw him come out of the front door. I drove to meet him and we left to return to my home. It was too late to go to church.

As we walked into the dining room, he said he had something to show me. He pulled out his billfold and showed me fifty dollars that he had hidden in the billfold. His face was shining as he told me that he had hidden it from his mother.

She had given him some of his money when they were in New York, but when they returned home, she took what was left away from him.

He said he wanted to use it to buy me an engagement ring and wanted me to take him to buy it. He didn't realize that he could not buy a ring for fifty dollars. This was part of the illness. He had lost the ability to put some things in prospective.

I agreed, but then couldn't figure out how I could pay the difference in the price of the ring and his fifty dollars without him finding out. Since he looked totally normal and acted the same way, the jeweler would not understand and I couldn't explain it without John knowing.

Then I thought about an online website that sold simulated diamond jewelry. We went to the computer and pulled up engagement rings. We looked at many rings. Some he said he didn't like right away; some he was not sure of.

We looked at some of the same ones many times until finally he said, "That is the one." It was a beautiful one-carat solitaire. The price was $105.00, but I didn't show him the price. We ordered it and until this day I think it is the most beautiful thing I own. It was a wonderful day filled with love and stories about his trip.

After a while his mother called and asked to speak to him. She was furious and told him to come home and that if he did not come home right then, he could never come back to her house.

He told her he wasn't coming home. She asked to speak to me and repeated her threat. She also told me that they thought that if they separated us by taking him to New York State, that he would forget me.

I asked her why she did not want him to spend time with me. She told me that after he came home from visiting me that he would ask a lot of questions about his money from the sale of his property.

I explained to her that he would talk to me about his money and his things and that when he did, he would often put his face in his hands and would cry from frustration.

I told her that the only thing I could do was to tell him that he should ask her about these things and that he had a right to know. She didn't give me any information and just said I needed to bring him home right then. He did not want to go.

I normally took him home on Sunday about six o'clock after we finished an early dinner. I hoped that after she had spent the day thinking about it, she would let John come back to her home. She knew he didn't have his medicine and how important that was.

I was wrong. When John called to tell her that he was coming home. she said he could not come back.

Now I had to figure out what to do. Of course, he was very happy, but I knew he had to have his medicine. If he could not go home, he could not get his medicine.

CHAPTER 7
Trip to Florida

I was going to leave the next day to go to Jacksonville, FL to a school to learn a new computer system that our organization was going to activate soon. I had to go and I had to learn it well. I was expected to come back and share what I learned with my co-workers.

His daughter and his sister were both out of town so there was no one to leave John with. My heart sank, but I could not let him know that he was presenting a problem for me. Somehow, I had to take him with me.

He could not be without his medicine, not even for a day and certainly not for a week. I asked John if he knew who his doctor was and he replied that, of course he did. He was not just his doctor, he was his fishing buddy. That gave me hope.

The next morning, we went to see his doctor and explained the situation. They enjoyed seeing each other and the doctor was very surprised to see him with me. The doctor gave John some medicine out of his sample supply. He carefully explained to me what the medicine was for and how it should be taken. I felt like I could finally relax and go to the next step.

I called my supervisor and explained the situation and that his daughter was out of town on vacation. There was no one for him to stay with. I asked if I could take him with me.

The people I worked with were very aware of what my situation with John and his mother was and they were very supportive of what I was trying to do to take care of him.

My supervisor said it was alright with her and suggested that I talk to my co-worker, Jean. Jean and I were going to school together and had planned to ride together. I asked Jean if we could all ride together and she quickly agreed.

Monday afternoon we started to Jacksonville. My stomach was in knots I was so worried about how I was going to manage all we were going to face once we arrived at the military base where the school was being held.

We enjoyed the ride. Jean had met John and she enjoyed talking to him. During the whole trip which was about five hours, my mind raced. I knew I could get him on the military base because the car had a decal and our country was not in a heightened state of security so they wouldn't check everyone in the car. I was sitting in the front seat, Jean was driving and John was sitting in the back seat.

Still, as we approached the gate, my heart beat very fast with anxiety. We had an identifying decal on the front of the car. We stopped at the gate and the guard came to the window of the car. Jean showed her identification and I was taking mine from my billfold. The guard glanced at John in the back seat and then waved us on through the gate. I breathed a sigh of relief.

He was a veteran of the Air Force so he had some right to be on a military facility.

My next concern was what to do when we got to the Visiting Officers Quarters (VOQ). Jean and I had separate rooms reserved, but should I declare that John was with me or should I just check in while he waited in the car. We weren't married so I couldn't say my husband was with me. I chose not to say anything, but I didn't feel good about this. One day at a time and a lot of prayer.

Jean and I checked in at the desk of the VOQ. It appeared that it had once been a barracks that has been converted to Visiting Officers Quarters. We were instructed that our rooms were at the end of a long hall and that there was a door and a parking lot at the end of the building so we drove around and went in that door with John and our luggage.

The building was an old gray building and all of the suites opened onto a central hall. The doors all looked exactly alike except for the numbers on the doors. The suite consisted of a small living room with a TV, a couch and a desk for studying. There was a large bathroom and a bedroom with a double bed. Not fancy at all, but adequate and comfortable.

A maid would come every day to clean the room. Was that going to be a problem with John there? He looked and talked absolutely normal so maybe it would be alright. He was also quite charming.

Next, I wondered if he could understand and remember that he was to stay in the room until I came to take him to lunch. The building was next to a river and that would be so tempting. What would happen if he went outside and got lost?

I put my name and where I was in school in his pocket so that if this happened and he was picked up by the military police for any reason they could find me. I would just have to face the consequences if there were any. At least he was in a safe environment. The fact that he was an Air Force veteran would be in his favor.

Every morning I made sure he was bathed and dressed before I left for school. If he did run into a problem during the day, I wanted him to make a good impression. I felt like he could hold his own with any conversation if he had a chance to do that.

I can't remember what we did for breakfast, but there was a small refrigerator there so maybe we had something in there to eat. That is where we kept his coco colas and snacks to have during the day.

I went to school every day, but was worried sick about how he was and what he was doing. This was the year 2000 and before everyone had a cell phone. Every time we took a break from the class, I tried to use the only phone available to the students. Other students needed to use it, too, but usually, if I waited long enough, I was able to call him to see how he was doing. He was always fine. That was John, always fine.

Without a doubt, I had to learn what I was there to learn because when I went home, I had to be ready to use what I had learned and teach others. I had to stay calm and concentrate, but it was hard.

Every day at lunch, we went back to the VOQ to get John and the three of us went to lunch at a little place on the base. The grounds were lovely and well kept. Moss hung from big oak trees and the bright pink of the Azelia bushes brightened up the lawn.

The dining room of the little restaurant had many windows and the food was good so lunch was a lovely experience.

After lunch, we took John back to the VOQ and I walked him to the door of our suite. Since all of the doors looked exactly the same except for different numbers, I wanted to make sure he went into the right door.

This presented another problem. What if he went into the hall for some reason and then did not know which door was our door?

One afternoon, we went to the commissary which is like a department store on the base. Since we were visitors, we were allowed to shop there. The prices there were very good.

As we walked in, John was walking right behind me as we headed down an aisle toward the middle of the store. As we walked along, I realized he had stopped.

I turned around. He had stopped at the lingerie section. Near the aisle was a rack of gowns. He had taken the bottom of a beautiful beige colored silk gown and was holding it to his face.

When I walked back to him, he said he wanted to buy that for me. Even though he had no money at that time, I always let him think he was paying for things. That was very important to maintain his personal dignity.

The last afternoon that we were there, I called John to say we were coming back early. As we pulled into the parking lot, he came bouncing out of the back door. I immediately wondered if he had left the room other times and, if so, how he found his way back to our rooms.

I soon found the answer, he had left the door open so he would know which door was ours. His memory was fading, but part of his brain was still working very well. I always reminded myself of this.

Somehow, we had made it through the week. Near the end of the week his sister, Rachel, found out where we were and called our room. She was furious and accused us of running away to Florida like a couple of high school kids.

She would not listen to what actually happened and said things that were very hurtful to me and to him. She said that she would "deal with us" when we got home.

I was not used to being talked to in this way and it really upset me. It was not that I was afraid of her, but that her attitude was so demeaning. I was already drained from worry and anxiety.

After we got home, his sister, Rachel, called to say that she and her husband were coming over to my home. I called my daughter and told that I thought she should be there. She came right over. I can't remember if John's daughter was there or not. I know she would have been if she was back in town.

My home was two stories. As you came in the front door, there was a small entrance way and then you had the option of going straight up the stairs or left into the dining room. You could turn right and go into the great room.

His sister and her husband came in the front door full of anger and harsh words. His sister was tall like John, probably close to six feet tall and was not a thin person. She had a very pretty face and her eyes, like John's and his mother's eyes, were very dark almost black. Her husband was large, too, so they made a very ominous appearance. I stepped up on the first step of the stairs to give them plenty of room. Being only 5' 5", I felt a little dwarfed so maybe it was a feeble attempt to level the playing field. We never moved from the front hall.

Obviously, his mother had failed to tell her that she would not let John come home and would not give him his medicine. John took up for me the best he could. He told her that he loved me and wanted to be with me.

After a long, unpleasant conversation, his sister said they would go to their mother's house and get his medicine and clothes and he could stay with me. I am not too sure that this was not the plan before they came, but that was fine with me. If I had not wanted him, I would not have let him stay.

CHAPTER 8
Together at Last

He was mine now to love and care for and only with the grace of God was I going to be able to do it. I had to keep working. Was he going to be able to stay at home by himself during the day? His mother had his money from the sale of his property. What about the cost of his medicine and doctor's visits?

We were not married so would the doctors talk to me about his health? All I could do was pray and this was my prayer. "Lord, I know that you have sent me to care for John and I will do it with all my heart, but I cannot do it alone. Please be with us wherever this terrible disease takes us and give me the strength to do your will. I love John, but I am not in love with him. Fill my heart with so much love that I can give this love to him. In Christ's blessed name I pray. Amen"

This was the beginning of a long journey filled with challenges, anxiety, hurt and frustration. It was also filled with love, fun times and lots of laughter. If there is anything that I can share with anyone else facing this situation that will help them get through each day, I want to do that.

Monday morning was coming fast. I would have to go to work, but what would happen to John? Could he stay by himself all day in our house? He had been able to stay in the VOQ on the Navy Base by himself all day and that was more of a challenge.

I had been reading everything I could find about dementia and I had talked to his neurologist trying to understand about how it affects the mind beyond short-term memory.

I learned that it was a progressive disease that spreads slowly through the brain. So, to my simple way of thinking, part of the brain would be normal before the disease spread to it.

I needed to know how much of cognitive ability was still okay. We had established that he remembered me and how we felt toward each other. He recognized other people, he could still read a little and even write a little. He still smiled and joked and was very sure he wanted us to be married.

He had remembered to leave the door to our suite at the VOQ open so he would know which door to go back into since they all looked the same. That showed he could think things out to some degree.

He knew he had money from the sale of his property, but he didn't know how much or where it was other than that his mother had control of it.

After having a life again, it was like pouring water on a sponge. John had gained weight and even the muscles in his body had returned to their original shape. I thought that was strange, but some of the men I worked with said that was called, "muscle memory".

He was a very handsome man, but the best part was that he had the same kind and loving personality. It was easy to fall in love with him all over again.

We had to talk about Monday and if he could stay alone while I went to work. He said that, of course, he could and didn't know why I was concerned.

We went over the details about how he should not leave the house while I was gone and if he went outside, he must be careful not to lock the door behind him. He understood this or at least said he did.

I had a telephone with large numbers and I wrote down the number where I worked. He knew he could call me whenever he wanted to. We practiced this and he did it very well.

We said we would prepare his lunch every morning before I went to work and leave it in the refrigerator. He reminded me he could use the microwave, but we agreed that he should not use the stove. We both loved coco cola so there was always plenty of that in the refrigerator. There were

Patricia Sanderfer

cookies and other snack foods. His favorite cookies were Oreos. When we went to the store, he always made sure we bought Oreos and Wheat bread.

His mother had told me that he had a drinking problem. We did not drink alcohol together, but there was wine in the house. I had to know if I needed to get rid of it so I left a bottle of wine that had about 2 inches of wine in the bottle in the refrigerator. He never touched it so we had answered that question. He did not have a drinking problem.

Every morning, before I went to work, I made sure he had a shower and was completely dressed. If he had any contact with another person during the day, I wanted him to look nice.

No one could tell by looking at him or talking to him briefly that he had a problem at all. I was always afraid someone would try to take advantage of him if they thought he was impaired in any way.

Actually, he could mostly dress himself after I laid out his clothes for him. He had perfect balance. He could stand in the middle of the room and put his socks on without sitting down. I thought that was amazing.

I would turn his undershirt and shorts in the right direction before he put those on. I probably did more than I needed to, but I enjoyed doing it. We would laugh and joke so he would not be conscious that I was "helping" him because he could not do it. Keeping his pride and self-esteem was always in my mind. He deserved no less than that. He was only 54 years old.

He always reminded me to put the television on his favorite channel and, after many kisses, I would leave to go to work leaving my heart there with him.

On the way to work, I would pray that God would look after him and that would ease my mind.

He usually called me several times a day. He could always get the first numbers right, but sometimes not the last two. Since we had rotary phones at work, his call might come in on someone else's phone. They would come and get me with a big smile on their faces. John is on my phone, they would say. So, I would go to their desk to talk to him briefly. Everyone was so kind to him. That made me feel so good.

One day John called me at work and he was very upset. He said his mother had just called and said his disability social security claim had been denied. I asked him if he was sure and he said he wrote down what she had told him. I told him to try not to worry about it and we would see about it when I came home. Obviously, his mother had filed a claim for him some time in the past. I did not know anything about it.

I called John's daughter to see what she knew and she did not know about the claim either. She said she had a friend at the Social Security office and she would call her to see what she could find out.

She called back in a little while and said there had been a claim filed, but it had been approved. The claim indicated that he lived with his mother and the mother had said that the payment should come to her home. His daughter told the representative from the Social Security office that he did not live with his mother anymore and that all of his expenses were being paid by me.

I took him to the bank and we opened a bank account in his name so his Social Security benefits could be deposited there. Now, he had money of his own and he knew where it was. It was not much because when he worked for the government as an air traffic controller, he had not paid into social security.

John's teeth were in very bad shape. He carried a tube of pain medication designed to stop a tooth ache in his pocket all of the time to be used when his teeth hurt.

I worried that it should not be used frequently and might be bad for his health. He needed to go to the dentist and that would be very expensive. His Social Security check was only a little over $700.00 a month and that would not begin to pay for the work he needed to have done.

Again, I talked to his daughter. If his mother still had money from the sale of his property, she should let him have enough money to take care of his medical expenses.

We began to ask his mother about his money. He also wanted to know where his boats and camper were so we asked about them.

His daughter and her husband had spent a lot of time and money on his big boat making repairs, but they had no idea what had happened to his boats or the camper because the land had been sold without her knowing about it. We could not get an answer from our questions.

When John's daughter and I went to the county where John had lived and looked at the sale of his property in the courthouse records, we had seen that the property had been sold to the person whose property adjourned John's property for only a fraction of what it was worth. Neither the boats nor the camper were included in the sale.

I can't remember exactly how it came to be that we were going to meet with an attorney to settle these matters. John's mother made the arrangements. The attorney's specialty was Elder Care or something like that. I did know that John would be paying the attorney's fees.

Even though I had worked as a court reporter in this county and knew most of the attorneys, I did not know her. I don't know what had been said to the attorney prior to the meeting.

The attorney took the role of being an arbitrator in the meeting and laid down some rules in the beginning. First, she would not let John sit beside me so he sat at the end of the table. His daughter was between us.

I don't remember exactly how the attorney phrased it, but she indicated that at any time she could ask anyone to leave the room if she was not happy with them being there.

Another rule was that no one was to interrupt her, but should make notes and ask questions at the end of what she had to say. This put John at a huge disadvantage because of his inability to make notes and his short-term memory problems.

My stress level was rising, but I was afraid to say anything because I thought she was just waiting for an opportunity to ask me to leave the room. This would be added stress for John.

I can't remember what preempted this, but I remember a time when John stood up and said, "I want to marry her." The attorney said, "You want to marry who? Her? And pointed at his daughter." He said, of course not, that he wanted to marry me.

Finally, we got around to the money. His daughter and I knew what his property sold for, but we just listened and did not contest the amount stated. John's mother had presented a bill for the five months he had stayed with her and some other bills. Nothing was said about the money spent on the trip or on the purchase of a car for a family member.

The bottom line was that there was about $20,000.00 or a little more left of money that belonged to John. When it was given back to John, it was deposited into his bank account. His daughter's name was put on the bank account with his. He was so happy to get some of his money back. Thank goodness, he didn't understand everything.

I could pull his account up on the computer for him to see. He would ask how much money he had. I would show him on the computer and he was very happy. This helped him keep his feeling of independence and his dignity.

Several times he mentioned that he would like to have his own car. I understood this. He would ask if he had enough money to buy a car and I always told him that he did.

He did not know that he no longer had a driver's license. I had taken him to the driver's license bureau and got him an identification card that looked like a license. There was no reason for him to know that he could not drive.

When the subject of him buying a car came up, I asked him what kind of car he wanted. He could not think of an answer to that question so I told him to think about it and when he decided, we would talk about it again. This would satisfy him for the moment and then we would go on to another subject. He could not live in my world so I had to live in his... always.

Now we had enough money to get his teeth fixed, but could he go through that? I went by the dentist office and talked to the dentist while John was not present. The dentist said he was willing to try.

John was anxious to get his teeth fixed so he was pleased to go to the dentist. As we sat in the office waiting for his appointment, I kept wondering what would happen. Could he remember to keep his mouth open? Would he be afraid? Should I ask to go in there with him and could I stand to watch?

Finally, a pretty young dental assistant came to get him acting very cheerful. He responded to her attitude and went willingly to the dentist chair. I remained in the waiting room and prayed. I didn't hear any unusual noises and after a long time, he came out smiling. I could breathe again.

We set up more appointments. It took several months little by little until finally his teeth were all fixed and the bill was paid out of his money. No more tooth aches. What a blessing and he had a beautiful smile.

John did not like his neurologist very much. The doctor would ask him questions and ask him to do things that sometimes John could not answer or do. This was necessary, but it made John uncomfortable.

On one visit, the doctor asked me if John could come to visit a class from the medical college where he taught. He wanted the class to see how well John could walk and act even though his brain was impaired. John was younger than the normal person who suffered from dementia so this was good for the students to see.

I left it up to John. I am not sure he totally understood, but he finally agreed. I also mentioned it to his mother and his daughter and they thought it was alright if the doctor would be careful to not embarrass him. The doctor assured me that neither he or the students would make him uncomfortable.

We arrived at the school and I could tell that John was a little anxious, but seemed alright. If he became too anxious, we would just leave.

The doctor asked John to walk across the room for the class to see how well he could walk. One of the questions the doctor asked John was what he had on his arm and pointed to John's watch. John looked up at him and said, "The same thing you have on yours." The class all laughed. I don't know if John could not recall the word watch or if he was being smart with the doctor. He was a master of cover up.

My daughter, her husband and their two daughters lived within five minutes of where we lived. That was wonderful for me because I could see them often and we were very close. As my granddaughters were growing up, we spent many happy hours together. They called me Nana as did many of their little friends who visited me with them. The friends still call me Nana if I happen to see one of them.

When John came to live with me, my granddaughters were curious, of course. They were now about 11 and 13 years old. I had never in my life lived with a man that I was not married to and felt a little guilty about this. In the year 2000 this was not a common practice. I took some of his shaving things and put them in the other upstairs bathroom, but I don't think I fooled them too much.

They were not overjoyed about him living there because all of their lives, I had been devoted to them. Now, I had someone else that took up so much of my time. Maybe they were too young to understand that just because I loved him, did not mean that I loved them any less. There was someone else living in the house they had considered almost a second home since they were very young.

One day at work I got a call from my oldest granddaughter. She said, "Nana, Angel is having a puppy." They were expecting the puppy and had prepared a large cardboard box with the front cut out of it. There were newspapers in the bottom of the box.

I asked her if Angel was in the box and she said she was. My granddaughter was very excited and worried. I told her Angel will be alright and Angel knew what to do with the puppy, but to let me know if there seemed to be a problem. She calmed down and hung up the phone. In a little while, she called back and said, "There is another puppy coming out." I assured her that was great; two puppies would be a good thing.

Patricia Sanderfer

CHAPTER 9
A Puppy for John

Angel was a Bichon Frise and like their mother, the babies were beautiful. Two little white balls of fur crawling all over each other and their mother. What an incredible and wonderful thing birth is and how blessed we were that they were healthy and perfect. Angel did indeed know what to do and she was a good mother. The puppies grew fast and were a delight to watch. They decided to keep the smallest puppy and sell the other one.

I began to wonder if having a puppy would be a good thing for John to keep him company in the daytime while I was at work. He enjoyed playing with them and would get down in the floor with them.

We talked it over and he was excited about having one of the puppies. I worked it out with my daughter and finally Angel's Beautiful Girl came to live with us. I called her Beauty, but John called her Baby Dog.

Bichons are adorable little dogs who love to sit in your lap and be loved. She was hard to house-break, but other than that, she was incredible. We agreed that John could take her outside to urinate, but that he must be very careful to bring her back into the house.

Looking back, I am not sure the puppy was a good idea because he took the responsibility so seriously. I do think that a pet is a wonderful idea for people who are ill or have dementia, but only if there is someone else there to share the responsibility of caring for the pet.

I have pictures of the two of them together and the sheer joy on his face. One picture that I treasure is a picture of John sleeping in our bed and Beauty, who was very tiny then, was curled around the top of his head sound asleep, too.

One day he called me at work. He said that he could not find the Baby Dog. He had looked and looked but could not find her. He said he had taken her outside, but he was sure he brought her back into the house. He was so upset that I thought he was going to cry.

My supervisor was sitting near where I sat and said, "Go home and help John find the baby dog." So, I left and started the 20-minute drive home. I hoped we would find the puppy, but what would this do to John if we could not find her. Could he deal with loss and maybe thinking it was his fault?

I pulled carefully into the driveway looking all around as I drove. I did not want to hit her with the car, but I did not see her anywhere. I came into the house through the garage. From the door I could see down the hallway into the great room.

As I entered the door, she crawled out from under the couch in the great room yawning. She had been asleep. I don't know which of the three of us was the happiest, John, me or the baby dog. We hugged each other and hugged her. Once again, all was well. One day at a time.

CHAPTER 10
A New Neurologist

The house next door to us sold to a neurologist. This was a blessing for us. Since John didn't like the man who was his neurologist at the present time, I thought there was potential there. I watched as the two of them talked and laughed when they were in the yard at the same time and so I asked her if she would accept John as a patient. John and I were both very happy when she agreed.

Not only did she observe and run tests on him at her office, there was the added benefit of her being able to observe him in the yard. He often helped me with the yard work.

We had a riding lawn mower and I enjoyed cutting the grass myself, but I could not let John drive this little tractor and he never asked to drive it. Instead, we had a small gas-powered mower that he could push and he liked to do that. The yard was divided by the driveway and we decided which part would be his area to cut.

This usually worked out for about 15 minutes and then I would see him and the little mower coming across the driveway toward where I was. I would just turn the mowers off and we would both go into the house. It was not safe for him to be near the large mower, because it occasionally hit a rock that could have been slung in his direction. Also, poor dear, he was in my way, but he could not know that.

Paramount in my mind at all times was that he not be aware of his limitations if I could help it. There was no reason for him to experience this hurt. It would serve no purpose in his care or his health. We never discussed the fact that his diagnosis was dementia, even though he had heard it many times.

His new neurologist, said the diagnoses could not be positive without doing a biopsy of the brain and we didn't want to do that. She said it would serve no purpose because the treatment for dementia is the same for both types. So, we carried on one day at the time.

Most of our social life centered around our church. There were parties, including dances, associated with that. He loved to dance and he loved people. He danced very well to slow music. There was only one small problem. When we danced he like to give me little kisses. One, occasionally. would have been wonderful, but sometimes he gave me too many kisses and this was a little embarrassing. No need to mention this to him. He would not understand. When we were at home, there were never too many kisses.

Most of his social graces were correct, but occasionally there were some things that were not right. One time we were at a reception and there was a long table of finger foods. Instead of putting a little of the things he liked on his plate to take back to our table, he would put several of the things he liked on his plate and then start eating them while we were going down the line. This, of course, slowed up the line of guests waiting to get their food to my dismay, but I had to remember that he could not live in our world, I had to live in his with love and understanding.

He could sing the hymns in church even though he did not try to read the words in the song book. The words were in his memory and he sang out loud and clear, loving every minute of it. I wondered if music was stored in a different part of the brain from regular memory or if it was because the songs were part of his long-term memory. Just a thought, but not important to me. We still have so much to learn about this disease, but a cure is the most important thing we need.

We agreed to do the "outreach program" in our Sunday School class. That meant we would do things for the community in the name of the church. Fall was coming and everything was beautiful. A children's home sponsored by the church was having an open house. The president of our class volunteered our class to do decorations for the children's home. This was an outreach project.

We took up a collection from the members of the class to cover some of the expenses and we got about $50.00. I knew we could do a good job with that because we were just responsible for the entrance to the main building.

As it turned out, the children's home expected us to decorate every building on the outside including a playground area where they had games set up. All I could do was pray because I had no idea how we could do that.

My prayers were answered. John and I had been to a fair in a neighboring town and I remembered seeing pots of beautiful flowers all over the fair grounds. I called the fair ground officials and asked if they would be willing to donate the flowers and any other decorations they could, to the children's home. I offered to pay a small amount. They agreed.

I didn't know how we would get the decorations from the fair grounds to the children's home, but I learned about another volunteer and she and her husband volunteered to take a truck and to go with us. He and John loaded the truck full of hay bales, pumpkins and flowers. When I took my check book out to pay for the flowers, I was told that they were free for the children. What a happy day. Our prayers had been answered more than we had ever expected.

When we returned to the children's home, we began to place our treasures around the grounds. The pots of chrysanthemums in shades of yellow and a red so deep that is was almost brown sitting on a bale of hay and surrounded by pumpkins gave the grounds of the children's home a festive fall atmosphere.

John was a huge help with this because he was so agile and strong. He could carry the plants and pumpkins with no effort at all. Of course, he loved what we were doing for the children.

Near the end of the long day, we were all a little tired. John could not always understand where I wanted him to put things and sometimes, I had to ask him to move something a couple of times. He never seemed to mind.

A woman was standing close by and she said, "I don't know who I feel most sorry for, him or you." This shocked me, but reminded me to be more tactful even though I was very tired. I turned to the woman and said, "We do not want your pity, but we would appreciate your prayers."

There would always be people around and I had to learn to accept that they would not always understand. There were many things I could have done better.

The next opportunity to do something big with the Community Outreach program for our Sunday school class was Christmas. This was also the first Christmas for John and me as a couple so we were already excited about celebrating Christmas together.

The class had adopted a family, a mother and her five children to provide Christmas for. There was no father living in the home and there would be no Christmas without help from somewhere. We were pleased to have the opportunity to help them in Christ's name.

We asked each child and the mother to make a list of things they would like to have for Christmas. There were about fifty members of the class so we felt confident that we could provide many of the things on the lists. Different people chose a child to buy for. Usually two or more people chose the same child and they worked together to get the items on the list. One little boy wanted a bicycle and this was a group effort to get that for him.

Christmas drew near and people starting reporting on their shopping efforts. There was only one problem. A toy on the smallest girl's list was nowhere to be found. It was that one toy that appears each year that every child wants so it sells out early. This made me very sad. She had not asked for much, some clothes and the toy.

Then one day, a store announced that they were getting a shipment of that toy in and they would go on sale at eight o'clock on Saturday morning, first come, first served.

John and I planned to be there when the store opened. What if the line was very long and they sold out before it was our time to make a purchase? We couldn't let that happen. I called the store manager and explained the situation. He agreed to hold the toy for one hour, but if we were not there, they would have to sell it.

We awoke early, dressed, and headed across town to the store. Snow was very rare in our part of the state, but there was a soft snow falling that morning. We had Christmas songs playing on the car radio so we were very happy. We were going to get the toy and the little girl would get her wish.

When we arrived at the store, we jumped out of the car and ran across the parking lot with the soft snow falling on our heads. My worst fear was true, there was a very long line of people waiting to buy THE toy. Should we go to the counter and identify ourselves so we could purchase the toy. I thought this would not be the thing to do. We would be breaking in line and that could cause one of those shopping scenes turned bad, so we waited at the end of the line.

After a while, the line began to disburse. They had sold out of the toy. We were still within our hour so we cautiously approached the check-out counter and told them that we had called the manager and arranged for a toy to be saved for us. In a few minutes the toy arrived and we made the purchase. What a time of joy. I was quite sure I could hear the Angels sing if only in my head and in my heart.

Finally, the big day came to give the gifts to the family. The room the class met in had one time been a chapel when the church was first built so there was a small stage, once a pulpit, at the end of the room. Some of the members had put a Christmas tree on the stage and gifts in bright colored paper were all around the tree. There was the bicycle with a big red bow standing off to the side of the tree. Many of the children had asked for clothes and shoes and those wishes had been granted along with games and toys.

We all waited anxiously as someone escorted the mother with her five children into the room. Their eyes were as big as saucers when they saw the presents and the mother began to weep with joy.

The presents were handed out one by one to the children and they began to open them. Looks of disbelief and joy filled their faces when they saw that all of their wishes had come true. Dolls were held to the little girl's chests and little cars and trucks were filling the floor. The larger boy just stood beside his bicycle touching it and then taking a step back to admire it once more. A boy and his bicycle, what fun lay ahead for them. Maybe he could get a newspaper route to help with the finances of the family.

My eyes and John's kept going to the littlest girl and to the mother. We were sure the mother was aware that the toy she wanted was sold out almost everywhere. It was the last package she opened and the look on her face made it all worthwhile. She cried with joy.

It was the best Christmas I had ever had and I have had many wonderful Christmases in my lifetime. In Acts 20:35, the Lord Jesus himself said: "It is more blessed to give than to receive."

Getting ready for Christmas this year was easier because John could help me with the decorations and go with me to do the shopping. I could tell it was getting a little harder for him to figure out how things fit together, but we had plenty of time and the fun of doing it together.

Under our feet was the baby dog getting into every open box and loving every colored paper that hit the floor. It was hers to tear into little pieces. We had to be careful what we dropped. Our baby dog was now a full-sized dog, but John still called her Baby Dog.

We put a baby gate between the kitchen where we kept her food and water and the rest of the carpeted house. We always put her in the kitchen when we left home, but when we returned, she would always be in the hallway to greet us. How did this little dog get over that gate? There was no way to get through it.

One day, we put her in the kitchen and went into a part of the house where she could not see us. We kept peeping down the hall and sure enough, she climbed up and over the gate. At the top she jumped to the floor. We were amazed. John was delighted at her skill and strength, but I was not as happy. No need to scold her, she just wanted to be free. We removed the gate from the door because we were afraid she might hurt herself. She was not our dog, we were her family.

Our life had begun as a couple and it was wonderful and complicated. There are some advantages of living with someone who has short-term memory. Often, he would come to where I was in the house and take me in his arms. He would say, "I don't believe I have told you today how much I love you." Every time he did this, I would act like it was the first time, too. How many years had we wished for this?

The holidays were over and the decoration were back in their boxes. Some of the boxes were stored under the stairwell. There was a little door on the back side of the coat closet that opened to that storage area, but you had to bend over to go through it and then you could stand up. This had always been difficult for me because of my arthritis, but it was easy for John. It was such a blessing that his motor skills were intact. He had total control of the use of his arms and legs.

What would Christmas next year be like? What was the coming year going to be like? No one can know those things, not just us, so we will enjoy every moment we have together and just take one day at a time.

CHAPTER 11
Our Wedding

One morning, John asked me when we were going to be married and why we were waiting. I answered that we had been waiting so we would know for sure if this was what we wanted to do. He said that he had asked me to marry him and I had said that I would. I was wearing his engagement ring.

I told him that I was sure that I wanted to marry him, but I wanted to be sure that he still felt that way after we had lived together for a while. He said that he had wanted to marry me for most of his life and that he wished we could do it now.

Why not, I thought, and I began to look at the reasons why and the reasons why not. Beyond the fact that we loved each other and planned to stay together, a really good reason was that I could add him to my federal health insurance and he needed that. Also, as his health declined and he needed more medical attention, I would be the next of kin and the doctors could discuss his illness with me. This had been happening so far, but we had a long way to go ahead of us.

Could we get a marriage license? Could he answer all of the questions the clerk asked him? I was not sure of that and I did not know if they would issue a license to a person with dementia.

My property, my home, would become John's, too. I was not sure what would be done to me when he died. Did I really want to be involved with anyone in a legal matter? We had to do this smart.

I had some software that had legal forms on it so I began to write a prenuptial agreement. Since I was going to be sure his life insurance stayed the same with his daughter being the beneficiary, I had to be sure that his burial expenses and any medical bills he accrued were paid out of that policy.

As hard and as cold as it seemed, I had to deal with the facts. We both needed to update our wills to reflect our wishes. After all, I could die before him. It was not likely, but it was possible. In that event, I would want anything I owned before John and I married to go to my daughter.

I finally had the papers written and I felt comfortable that everything would be fine. I would get a lawyer to look over them and we would sign them before witnesses in a legal way. Maybe, if he was not too busy and would not mind, I could ask a judge that I knew to look at them. I had worked for him many years ago as his court reporter and we had remained friends.

Also, I would like for the judge to talk to John to be sure that he knew what he was doing and that he wanted to marry me. I never wanted to be accused of marrying someone with dementia for any reason other than for love.

The people I worked with gave us a wedding shower in the office building where I worked. They knew our love story and had been very supportive during the time we were together. They had talked to him on the phone when he tried to call me and dialed the wrong number and were looking forward to meeting him.

John was excited to be going to the shower. He wanted to meet the people I worked with and see where I worked. There was a cake and refreshments and a lot of laughing and joking. It was a fun time for us.

Their present to us was a money tree. Different people had given bills in different value, $10,00, $20.00, $5.00 and they were folded, tied with ribbon and used to decorate a small tree that had no leaves, just limbs. John thought that was great idea and we had a lot of fun unfolding the bills when we got home. We used the money to buy a radio/CD player with large speakers that we actually used for the music at our wedding.

Next big step was to get the marriage license, because if we could not, if they discovered that John had dementia and decided he was not capable of making this big decision of marriage, they might not give us the license.

When I told John that we would go to get the license the next day, he was excited. I was a little excited, too. The license office was in the courthouse where I had worked as a court reporter for several years.

I loved that stately old building built with red bricks many years ago. The halls were huge and you could stand in the center hall and see all of the way to top of the fourth floor. The stair case wound its way to the top. The floors were white marble and the stairs were the same. Thank goodness there were also elevators. Huge doors of dark mahogany opened into offices and court rooms.

There was a door like that in what was once my little office that opened onto the hall, but the Judge instructed me to never unlock it or go in or out that way because sometimes prisoners got away from the guards and he was afraid they would see that as a place to run to. I was never tempted to do that. I respected the Judge. He was a great man, honest and fair with everyone.

We turned onto the street where the courthouse was and it was just as I remembered from my days there. The two streets were two lanes each going in one direction. The median that separated the streets was incredibly beautiful dressed out for Spring with Azelia bushes in pink and red nestled under the huge tulip trees with their purple and white blossoms. Little benches were scattered here and there on the freshly mowed green grass. They were empty now because it was morning.

The parking on that street was horizonal parking. If I found an open space, could I still park in a horizonal parking space? It had been a long time since I had done that and I was not sure.

We were about to find out, because there was an open space. I expressed my fear to John and he said that, of course, we could park here. Yes, I thought that he could have done that before he became ill, but I did not say that. After a few stops and starts and a lot of encouragement from John, I managed to get the car into the space.

We jumped out of the car and crossed the street. It felt good to climb the big steps and enter the courthouse. The license office was on the first floor. We were shown into a small room just big enough for a desk and two

Patricia Sanderfer

chairs. That was good, nothing to distract our attention. Behind the desk was a lady with a lovely smile and a kind face. So far, everything was good.

I was so relieved when she handed us a clipboard with some forms to fill out. She handed it to John. He thanked her and handed it to me. I knew the answers for me, of course, and most for him. I did not remember his mother's maiden name. Would he remember it. I had to take the chance.

I asked, "John, what was your mother's name before she married your father. He said, "grandma". That is what he called his mother. I said that I knew that was what he called her, but for this form we needed her real name and he said Elizabeth. As soon as I heard the name Elizabeth, I remembered the last name was Combs. Great, I said, Elizabeth Combs, is that right? He said that was right. I glanced at the lady and her expression had not changed. She kept smiling at John and for once I did not care. He was quite handsome and always smiling his big enchanting smile.

Soon it was over and we had the license. I felt so relieved. She also gave us a gift from the county that was a pretty blue bag containing some personal items.

As we left the office, there was an elevator right across the hall. I asked John if we could take the elevator up to the third floor where the judge's office was. He thought that was a great idea.

I was hoping the judge was in his office and was not busy. He was there and standing right inside the door as we entered the reception area of his offices. He was glad to see me like he always was and it was good to see him. He glanced at John and then saw the gift bag from the license office.

He asked if we were there for him to marry us. I laughed and said that we were not there to be married. I ventured to ask the next question. Did he have time and would he be willing to look at the prenuptial agreement and the wills I had written. He said he would be glad to and invited us into his office.

There was a quiet time as he looked over each document carefully. He said, "I always knew you were smart, but these are very good and I don't see anything wrong." I am not so smart, I told the judge. I had some software that had forms on it. Software and hardware were not everyday terms in the year 2001 so he just smiled.

I explained to him that I was afraid that someone would think that I was taking advantage of John because he had been diagnosed with dementia. He said that he did not see anything in the documents that benefited me and asked if I wanted him to talk to John. I was very pleased.

The judge and John went into an adjourning room and talked for a few minutes. This did not make me nervous, because I was confident how John felt. In a few minutes, they came out. The judge said, with a big smile, "There is one thing I am sure of. This boy wants to get married." The people in the judge's office signed as witnesses after John and I signed the forms.

As we left the courthouse, I felt like I wanted to dance and sing. I was going to marry the love of my life and everything was going to be alright. I don't even remember if it was hard or easy to get the car out of that parking space, because the whole world had taken on a beautiful glow.

Purple and white blossoms floated down from the Tulip trees, the park benches were full of happy people and children were playing in the grass. Our cup runeth over with the love of God. I felt like I could have floated home.

I looked at John. His normal big smile was more like a grin. "We did it", he said. I said, "Yes, we did and I am so proud of you."

Now John started asking about the wedding. Simple question for him, we should just get married. For me it was a question of how we should do this. With his family at such odds with each other, could we have a regular wedding? I didn't think so.

We planned a wedding for the weekend of Easter. We didn't want a big wedding, but we did want to be married in the church by a minister. On Easter weekend the church would be beautifully decorated in white Easter lilies and Easter is thought of as the time of new beginnings. This was certainly a new beginning for us. The church administrator said we could be married on Saturday before Easter Sunday.

We asked the associate minister, a lovely lady, if she would marry us. She agreed and said she wanted to talk to us first. I was very glad of that. This would be someone else who had talked to John and would know how coherent he was and that he wanted us to be married.

The three of us talked, but she talked more to John. I enjoyed the conversation. I was especially glad when she asked him about his faith in God. I knew he was a Christian and enjoyed going to church with me. He knew all of the songs without being able to read so I knew the wordship service was not new to him. I didn't know if he had made a public confession of faith. Was he doing that by saying to a minister now that he believed in God. I felt sure that counted if it was something he needed to do.

We explained we wanted a small wedding with just his daughter, Melody, her husband, my daughter, her husband and my granddaughters present. My brother would give me away, my daughter would be my matron of honor and John's son-in-law would be his best man.

There would be no reception. I was a member of the Officer's Club on the military base where I had previously worked so I had reserved a small dining room for all of the wedding guests. My daughter had offered to meet with a cake baker we had used before to design a small wedding cake. The cake maker would deliver the cake to the Officer's Club for our dinner.

I was also so excited that my brother was going to visit us and that he would give me away at the wedding. I was nine years older than him, but we had always been so close. I loved him so much. Because of the visits John and I made to visit him when he lived in Florida, they were already friends.

CHAPTER 12
The Wedding

Finally, the big day came. The wedding was not until the late afternoon so my brother invited John to ride with him to a small nearby town where my brother had grown up. He hoped to see some of his friends.

They were not gone very long and I expressed surprise that they were back so soon. My brother said John was too nervous about missing the wedding to enjoy the trip so he brought him home.

John's son-in-law, Steven, had taken him to get a haircut a few days before and the barber had cut his hair too short. His dark wavy hair with just a touch of gray was one of his best features, but he was still so very handsome in his new navy suit. He was excited, but did not appear to be nervous. He knew and I knew that his son-in-law would guide him through the ceremony. Everything was good.

Because it was a simple wedding, I chose a pretty, cotton, ankle-length dress in John's favorite color, green. It was enough because all brides, on their special day, seem to glow and are pretty.

His daughter, Melody, had a bouquet made for me and it was lovely in shade of creamy white and had a lot of roses in it. I loved it very much and her for doing that for me. I had become very fond of his daughter.

The aisle of our church is very long and as I started down the aisle toward where John was standing with his son-in-law, his daughter's husband, it seemed like all of the years before flashed across my mind and how long we had wanted to be together. Now it was finally happening and it was even sweeter because my brother was escorting me down the aisle.

The minister, knew John would not be able to repeat the marriage vows very well. She said, "John, repeat after me." Then she said a few words at a time so he could remember. Then he repeated the words. After a few words at a time we got through the ceremony. What a kind and wonderful person the minister was.

The ceremony was very emotional for us, because neither of us had ever dreamed it would actually happen. As I repeated my part, I could feel tears welling up in my eyes, tears of joy. I was standing facing John and I could see tears in his eyes, too. The minister later said she had never married any couple that cried. I explained to her that they were tears of joy following a lifetime of emotional happenings.

After the wedding, we were gathering in the narthex of the church getting ready to go to the Officers' Club for dinner when my daughter asked John and me to go with her. We entered a large room of the church and I could not believe my eyes.

My sister and her family had planned a beautiful reception for John and me and all of our friends and family were there. Looking around the room at the guests, I saw that my best friend for many years was there even though she lived in a different state. How had they managed to keep this from me? Obviously, they had been planning it for a long time.

My daughter had contacted the lady who was making the cake and had her add more tiers making it almost twice as large and very beautiful.

Everything was perfect with champagne glasses for toasting and a punch bowl for the other guests. The food was incredible and John's daughter had gotten beautiful flower arrangements made for the tables.

There were many delightful presents and we had a lot of fun opening them together.

After the wedding, we went back to our home and the next day my brother left to go back to his home in North Carolina. I was so glad to share this incredible time with him and so glad he and John were friends from the old Panama City days when we were dating over thirty years before.

My brother was very happy about our marriage even though none of us knew what lay ahead. One day at a time.

The next day, John and I left to go to Gatlinburg for our honeymoon.

I am not sure he fully understood where we were going, but he was definitely excited. Living in the moment, he was perfect and so much fun. The problem was the short-term memory, but that was only about certain things and not everything.

He knew we were married and we were going on a trip. He also knew that he was happy and that we were happy together. This was not totally bad because he didn't have to worry about anything. He seemed confident that everything would be fine.

We left in the morning and it took most of the day to get to Gatlinburg. Right before we arrived there, snow began to fall and it was sticking to the ground. We were going over a mountain and I worried a little about how the driving would be. He was not worried, of course, because he grew up in the state of New York and so this was very special to him. I would not have worried if he had been able to drive.

He asked if we could get out and enjoy the snow so I pulled over in a place by the highway designed for people to pull over and enjoy the view. I soon relaxed as we made little snow balls and threw them at each other. Watching the joy on his face overcame any apprehension I had about the snow. It was so much fun.

We made it over the mountain without a problem and soon arrived at our hotel. It was even more than I expected. It was built on the edge of a little stream and was very rustic with a huge stone fireplace on the first floor and a balcony where you could go out and enjoy the stream as it tumbled over the rocks.

So far everything was going really well. John was carrying our larger bags and we started up to our room in the elevator. We did not use a luggage cart. As we got off of the elevator on our floor, there was a man standing there with a flat luggage cart. I guess he was returning it to the lobby.

Without a word, John dumped our luggage on the cart the man had and then walked on with me. The man had a shocked look on his face, not angry but surprised. I turned around and apologized profusely to the man saying that John liked to joke. He laughed and offered us the luggage cart, probably glad he did not have to carry it down to the lobby. We accepted and thanked him.

John and I didn't discuss what had happened. There was no point, no lesson to be learned there and certainly no wrong doing. I went with him to take the cart back to the lobby saying I wanted to go out on the balcony and look at the stream again. We did exactly that and enjoyed every minute of it. It was not snowing now because we were in a valley so I was so glad we stopped on top of the mountain.

The room was designed for a honeymoon with a jacussi in the room. This was kind of wasted on us, well on me. John had always wanted us to shower together, but I would not. I was getting older and self-conscious about my body. I was more comfortable being under the cover and in a dark room. I sure was not going to get in a hot tub.

Now I am sorry, just as I knew I would be some day. I was 65 and he was 56. This had never bothered him, but sometimes it did bother me.

There was an outlet shopping center nearby and a good opportunity to add to his wardrobe. We went to a couple of stores and found some nice pants for him. As we left the last store, he said we were not buying anything else unless it was for me. He was very serious about this.

I saw a dress shop nearby so I suggested we go in there. My heart really wasn't in it because I already had too many clothes. I was looking at clothes in my size and he walked on to another part of the store.

In a few minutes, he came back with this very feminine pants suit, more like a blouse and pants. He had a big, proud look on his face and asked how I liked it. It was not in my size, but I told him that if we could find it in my size, we would buy it. He went to find a store clerk and brought her back to me. She looked around and found it in my size so I let him think he was buying it for me.

We had a wonderful time in this little town, more like a village, and ate some incredible food. After a few days we started for home carrying so many memories with us. I don't know how much he remembered, but I will remember them the rest of my life. It didn't matter if he remembered or not. He had enjoyed the trip and tomorrow would bring another day to enjoy. That is all that mattered.

Patricia Sanderfer

CHAPTER 13
John's Health

Now that we were married, I was able to add John to my federal health insurance even with his illness. No questions were asked. This increased my premiums because I went from self-only to self and family, but it was a blessing.

Now we were able for his neurologist to run the tests that she had been wanting to run, including an MRI and other expensive tests that we could not afford before.

John and I talked about the MRI, about how it was done and the purpose of it. I told him it was the best way for us to know how to make him get better.

We talked about it many times and then we went for our appointment for the MRI. The technician had been briefed about his condition so everything went smoothly. He explained to John about the loud noises he would hear and about how important it was for him to lay very still. Could he do this? Would he be frightened? We had to try.

I told John I would be with him all of the time. This always seemed to calm him. I asked the technician if I could go into the room with him and he said I could. He put a vest on me to protect me from radiation or whatever might not be good for me.

John cooperated completely and I held his hand for as long as I could. Soon it was over and the neurologist was later able to tell me what it showed. She said his brain had shrank away from his skull like that of a much older person. She used other medical terms that I did not understand and it didn't matter anyway.

She also mentioned that the only way to determine if it was indeed Alzheimer Disease or vascular dementia was to do a biopsy of the brain which could be dangerous and would serve no purpose because all dementia is treated the same.

Because of the tests and the unavoidable conversations with the doctors afterward, he became more aware of his new limitations. He had now been to my office and met the people so he wanted to go to work with me every day. I told him that was not possible, but he kept asking.

I asked him if he was becoming afraid of staying at home during the day while I was at work and he said, "Wouldn't you be after you heard what they said about me? I told him that I understood. It was interesting to know that he remembered what had been said.

I talked to his neurologist about her giving him something that would help him avoid becoming agitated when he couldn't do what he was trying to do. She asked me how important sex was to us. I said it was very important, but his feelings were more important. She said the medication would possibly affect his sexual feelings.

She gave him the medicine. I couldn't tell the difference right away and never knew through the coming months if it was the medicine or the illness when things slowly changed to a deeper, if less exciting, love.

I found that there was a place nearby where people who were unable to stay by themselves during the day while their caregivers were at work could stay. It was like an adult daycare and it was very nice. I could drop him off on my way to work and pick him up in the afternoon. This was the perfect solution and he seemed to like it there and liked the people.

He was handsome and charming and most of the people who worked there were women so he was very well accepted. The only problems he ever caused was interfering when a nurse was talking to a patient and the patient was crying. They told me he would come over and say, "Don't make her cry." He also pushed some of the people around in their wheel chairs. This was another answer to a prayer.

It was a little expensive, but now he had some of his money from the sale of his property to pay for his stay there. The local Alzheimer Association paid for one day of the week. That helped a lot.

Some of the people were permanent residents so they were fed three meals a day. John only ate lunch there. At least that is what he told me. We enjoyed eating breakfast together at home so we continued to do that and I was sure he was eating what he liked. He would not eat grits which is a Southern favorite.

When I picked him up in the evening, I asked if he had eaten dinner and he always said he had eaten a little, but it wasn't much. If I pushed a little and asked what he had eaten, he always looked out of the window of the car and said, "It wasn't much." That ended that conversation.

Most evenings we went somewhere for dinner. I would always ask him where he wanted to go. He used his charm and his ability to bluff his way around admitting that he did not know.

He always said, "I don't know and I don't care because I am with my baby." How could I not love this man?

After careful consideration, I decided to retire from my job. I loved my work as a Management Analyst. It was interesting and challenging, but I knew the quality time that John and I would have together was more important and that the days were numbered.

There was a lovely retirement ceremony where I was presented with a flag that had once flown over the capital building in Washington, DC. Following the ceremony was a reception given by the people I had worked with. John attended everything and enjoyed every minute of it, it seemed to me.

We were going to be home together every day and that would be wonderful. I would no longer have to worry if he was alright during the day.

I decided that John would continue to stay at the day care one day of the week. There were some things that it was difficult for me to do with him going with me and I could not leave him alone.

Another reason was that he was familiar with the day care and knew the people there. If it was ever necessary for him to stay there, he would be comfortable and they would know him.

After a few weeks of doing this, one of the men who worked there told me that John just stood in the hall all day waiting for me to come back and get him. I didn't know that and it broke my heart so I didn't take him back there anymore.

I loved our home. It was a Williamsburg style two-story home painted a soft blue-grey with white trim and black shutters. There was a large front yard and a wooded area in the back. I had lived there for ten years before John came to live with me.

There were many happy memories with my grandchildren visiting me there from the time they were very small. There were also memories of when John visited me there in earlier years although I don't think he remembered that. Not important, I remembered.

There was an anticipated problem with the house. That was the stairs going to the bedrooms on the second level. We had no problem with the stairs now, but I knew there would come a time when John could not go up the stairs and there was no bedroom on the first floor. As I got older, the stairs could be a problem for me, too.

A friend told me about a house in the neighborhood where she lived that would soon be available. She knew I admired this area and the house was all on one level.

Even before the house was listed, I asked he owners if I could see it. Reluctantly, they agreed because they were in the process of getting it ready to be sold. I asked if I could just walk through the great room into the dining area where I could see the back yard out of a huge window.

That was all I need to see, there was a creek running through the far edge of the backyard and many huge oak trees. It was perfect for John and me. He would enjoy sitting on the deck and feeling like he was outdoors. I would like that, too.

Our house sold in a month and we bought the new house. I was so excited to move in, but many unexpected things happened before we could do that. Our lives changed drastically.

CHAPTER 14
John's Illness Becoming Worse

John had a family member who was graduating from high school. His family wanted him to go to the graduation. He did not want to go. I asked his mother if he could stay with her the day of the graduation and then go with them that night. She said yes. I spent the day with my daughter. We went to Atlanta. I needed to spent some time with her. I had neglected my family.

That night, his family brought him to our home after the graduation. They were pretty upset with him. He had not wanted to stay at the ceremony and just wanted to come home. He rushed into the house and threw his arms around me. We were both tired so we went to bed early that night.

The next day, he was anxious and confused. He kept saying he wanted to see his family...that they didn't know where he was. I assured him that they knew where he was and told him that he had seen them the day before, but he could not remember.

He became more and more agitated and confused. He said he needed to find Pat and I could not convince him I was Pat. I was so afraid he would walk out of the house.

I called the doctor's office to see if they could call in a prescription to help him calm down. The office was closed, it was a Saturday, but another doctor had taken the call. He said he could not give him a prescription without seeing him first and the office was closed.

Finally, I called his daughter and she and her husband came over. They could help me if he tried to leave.

By now all he wanted to do was to find Pat. They tried to help him understand that I was Pat. We showed him a picture of him, me and my brother taken at the wedding. He said, there is another man in that picture beside him.

At one point he went halfway up the stairs and sat down on a stair. I stood at the bottom of the staircase and tried to talk to him to convince him I was Pat.

He said, "Why don't you leave me alone, I have a girl." This broke my heart. I asked him who his girl was and he said, "Pat".

After a long time, we all became pretty exhausted. His son-in-law asked him if Pat worked at the Air Force base. John said that she did. He asked him if Pat picked him up every day when she got off from work. He said that she did.

We called the daycare and asked if we could bring him there to spend the night and I would come to get him the next day. After we explained what was going on, they said that he could come. We hoped this would help him get back to a routine he remembered, back to reality.

The next morning, I went to get him. He obviously saw me from the front window because when I came through the door, he came bounding down the hall like always and threw his arms around me. I was his Pat again.

They told me that he had not slept all night and that he had stayed in the recreation room where the windows opened to the front of the building. He could see if someone pulled up to the front of the building in a car. It was all I could do to keep from crying, but I was so glad to have him back with me mentally. We went home and everything was good again.

On Monday, we went to his doctor, his regular family doctor. I told him a little about what had been going on, as much as I could in front of John. I had explained more when I asked to bring him in. I also told him that John had been extremely thirsty for the last week or so.

John and the doctor laughed and talked and the doctor checked his vital signs and seemed to think he was alright. For the moment, he was. They did not do a blood test or a urine test.

As we left the parking lot, he said he wanted to see his mother. I told him he had seen her a couple of days before, but he said he wanted to see her.

I called his mother and asked if she would let us take her to lunch. She agreed. She met us at the front door of her high-rise apartment building and we went to lunch at a family-style restaurant.

When the food came, we started eating. John was drinking more water than he was eating and his mother was more watching him instead of eating. She began to fuss at John for drinking too much water and not eating.

Finally, he stopped doing either. I finished eating and his mother was ready to be taken home. She was not very happy and we had not talked very much.

The next morning, we went to the lawyer's office to sign the papers to close on our new home. The parking spaces were in the back of the building which was located on a very busy street.

The lawyer's office was in a renovated older building and they had spent more on bricking the front and making it look professional than they had on the back. It was mostly white wood. There was a white wooden wheel chair ramp leading to the back door.

As soon as we got out of the car, John said he was not going in there. I told John that this was the lawyer's office and we had to close the sale on our new home. John said he was not going there. He said "grandma" had told him that I was going to put him in a hospital. He called his mother, grandma.

He kept looking at the street which was visible from the parking lot if you looked to the side of the building. The cars were zooming on the four-lane street very fast.

He would surely die if he tried to leave.

I called my daughter and her husband, who owned a printing company downtown, and asked if they could come help me with John. They were a full 15 minutes from where we were and, of course, they couldn't just run out and leave their business without some preparation.

The real estate agent who was selling the house was very anxious for us to come into the office where the attorney was waiting to close the contract. He tried to talk to John, but it was useless. It was pretty clear that John was looking for a way to get away. My daughter and her husband were not there yet.

Across the street from the real estate office was an ambulance service. The real estate agent suggested, we call them to come help us. I was desperate and didn't know what to do. Finally, I agreed. I could not postpone the closing because the seller was on her way out of town. She lived in another state many miles away.

When the ambulance arrived, the men on the ambulance knew how to talk to John and they convinced him to get into the ambulance. Then they asked me where they were going to take him. I immediately thought of the place where he had been staying in the daytime while I worked and told them to take him there. When my daughter and her husband arrived, they said they would meet the ambulance at the daycare and take care of anything that needed taking care of there.

After the closing of the property was over, I went to the facility where John had been taken. When I got there, my daughter told me that they had told her that he could not stay there.

The ambulance then took him on to the emergency room of a local hospital so he could get help.

I called John's daughter and she met me at the hospital emergency room.

It was horrible. On the way to the hospital, John had seen the tall hospital building and thought it was the high-rise apartment building where his mother lived. He became very aggressive, agitated and tried to get out of the ambulance. He was very strong so I understood why they had to constrain him.

When I got to the emergency room, he was still constrained with big leather straps and he was trying to get away. This was just causing the straps to dig deeper into body and in his struggle, he had slipped down to where they were in his groin area, too.

It was horrible to see him like this. I knew he was in so much pain. My darling, my darling, what can I do?

He just kept saying, "let me up."

I had promised myself when we had become a couple that I would never let anyone hurt him and there was nothing I could do. We tried to talk to him, but he just kept hollowing for us to let him be free. I am not sure he even knew who his daughter and I were.

The attendant said he thought we were making things worse and that we should let them take care of him. He said they would give him something to help him relax.

He was going to be taken to a senior care facility at another hospital so I went home until we knew he had been admitted there. My heart was breaking and I am not sure how I got home that day. All I could do was pray that God would take care of him.

Things were not good at the hospital. It had taken four men to put him in the bed, they told me, and the staff was afraid of him so he was not getting the care he needed.

They told me at the desk that he walked around a lot and that he was constantly touching his groin area. I knew he would never do that unless there was a reason. I suspected he had hurt himself in that area when he was strapped down and that he might also have a urinary tract infection. I had suspected that when he was drinking so much water previously.

I mentioned this to them at the nurse's station and they told me they were not going to try to get a urine sample from him. I asked them to give me something to collect it in and I would get the sample. I took him into the bathroom and successfully collected the sample.

I asked his doctor what the sample showed and he said there was a urinary infection, but it was not a really bad infection. My thought was that any infection was uncomfortable and bad.

He had two doctors attending him. One was a general practitioner and the other a psychiatrist. They told me that to be in that hospital, he had to have a psychiatrist. He had not needed a psychiatrist before so I did not know anyone. I looked in the list of doctors that participated with our insurance and picked the first name on the list.

This was a big mistake. I should have gotten references, but I was overcome with grief and was not thinking clearly.

On the psychiatrist's first visit, he looked at me and said John looked like Omar Shariff, the actor.

I could not tell the nationality of the doctor, but I hoped he was not from the part of the world where Afghanistan and Iraq were because we were at war with them at this time. I was just not comfortable with the way he looked at John or talked to him, but what could I do.

All John had were the dress shoes that he had worn to the lawyer's office. They were loafers that he could slide his feet into. He was able to get up from the bed and walk around the halls. His feet and ankles were so swollen that the shoes were soon terribly out of shape because he had rammed his feet into them. His stomach was swollen. I brought him some different shoes and some pants with elastic waistbands.

I wanted to stay with him all day every day, but I had to pack and be out of our house. I tried to get an extension, but the buyers had to be out of their house so I was not able to get an extension to the time we had to be out of our house. I got some help from my family, but they did not have much time to spare. I did not want to take everything to our new smaller home. I wanted to go through it and donate some things to charity.

The problem was daunting. Our 2300 square foot house had four walk-in closets and more storage space. They were all filled with "stuff". I would go the hospital every morning and then return home to pack.

Members of my Sunday School class came over and packed up the kitchen. That was a wonderful help and it also helped my feelings of despair. My granddaughters packed up my closet and my daughter and her husband helped as much as they could.

Sometimes I packed late into the night. I would become sick at my stomach from worry and a sense of hopelessness. I would sit on the steps of the deck on the back of the house. I would throw up on the ground so I wouldn't mess up one of the bathrooms.

Looking back on this, I wish I had just paid a moving company to pack the things in the storage areas and put them in the garage of the new house. It would have been very expensive to pack and move things I was going to get rid of, but my place was at the hospital with John. I thought he would be alright there with trained personnel, but he was not.

One day a person from the administrative office came to John's room and said they were going to dismiss him. The doctor had signed the orders. She wanted to know where he would be going.

I told her that they could not dismiss him, that he was very sick. I asked her to look at his abdomen and his ankles. They were swollen and you could tell by looking at him that he was sick. She said the psychiatrist said there was nothing more they could do for him.

I was afraid that if he left the hospital, he would die. This was before everyone had a cell phone and there was no phone in his room. I went to the end of the hall where there was a phone and called his neurologist. I explained the situation to her. She said that since she was not his doctor at the hospital, she could not come to the hospital, but that she would call the director of the hospital and talk to him.

Soon after that the other doctor who was supposed to be looking after John came to his room. He said he had not signed a directive for John to be dismissed. He examined John and said he would not be dismissed.

By morning, John had been moved to intensive care. He was suffering from a reaction to a drug called Haldol, according to his medical records. The medical staff could not tell me if he was going to live or not. He has to live, he cannot die. There was nothing I could do except pray.

He did not seem to be aware of whether I was there or not. Seeing him like this was almost more than I could take. He did not deserve to suffer like this and he did not deserve to be treated like a disease instead of a human being.

I was supposed to keep him safe and now I was about to lose him, but worse than that was the suffering he had gone through and was going through. Please, Lord, help us through this.

He lived. Thank goodness, he lived and was moved to another part of the hospital after a long stay in intensive care.

His doctor said he would have to have someone with him all of the time. I could not stay around the clock and there was noone else. The doctor said I would need to hire nurses to be with him when I could not be there. I told the doctor that it was their responsibility to have someone stay with him when I could not, because they had allowed him to get in this condition. The hospital complied. Even if the hospital charged for that service, our insurance would pay for it. They did not charge for it.

Part of the time I could leave the hospital and finish getting us moved. I had been having the new home painted on the inside before I brought him home because he could not be exposed to the fumes from the paint.

I was so glad that the new home was all on one level and there was a creek running behind the house. I was excited because I knew or hoped John would enjoy the creek as much as I would.

He had spent his life enjoying nature and from the deck on the upper level he could see tall oak trees, an occasional squirrel or rabbit and always the little chipmunks playing in the yard. Birds loved the area, too, and because the house was on the edge of a steep hill, the deck was even with the tree branches below.

How wonderful that would be to sit in our chairs and enjoy that together. Maybe we could hold hands again like we used to do.

Before we came home, my daughter contacted a locksmith and he came to our home and put deadbolt locks on all of the outside doors. They had to be opened with a key. This was absolutely necessary to keep him from wandering off and getting lost. The keys were hidden where he would not see them, but close to the door in the event of an emergency.

CHAPTER 15
Finally Home

Finally, we are home in our new house, but things were very different from before John went to the hospital.

I took one of the bedrooms and made a Memory Room for John like I had done in our last home. He had been a Bass fisherman and had several trophies from fishing tournaments. I put them on some shelves and hung a Bass fish that he had mounted over the trophies.

He also had a deer head mounted from a deer he had killed. It was beautiful, but I was glad he had decided to stop deer hunting even before he got sick. He said he had rather see them walking around. I hung the deer head on the wall.

He had several rifles. Two of them were guns that had belonged to his beloved grandparents, one was his first rifle and the others were his guns that he had used for hunting.

They were displayed in a pretty gun cabinet with a glass door that I had given to him on his last birthday. We did not have any shells for the guns.

There were other small things, like golf and baseball trophies that belonged to him, too. Each day, we would go into the room and talk about these things. Actually, I talked and he just looked at them intently and listened. We did this every day. I don't know what he thought because he never said a word.

Trying to make him comfortable with our new home, I took him to the large window in the back of the house. It was so large, it took up most of the wall so being in that room was almost like being outside.

From this view, you could look down on the little creek that ran behind the house. The house was perched on the top of a steep hill, but instead of enjoying the view, it seemed to make him uncomfortable. I was a little disappointed that he was not enjoying the view, but I hoped that, in the future, he would feel safe looking down.

We were able to sit on the back deck and enjoy the view from there. The deck had a railing and the chairs we sat in were rocking chairs that we had on the porch in our last house. All of this seemed to give him a sense of comfort.

The deck did not have a roof over it and I would observe his eyes searching the sky. He had always done this when we were outside. Was he checking the clouds with an eye of an outdoorsman or was it a habit from the days when he was an Air Traffic Controller? There was no way to tell because he never said anything.

We were contacted by someone who was a nurse/supervisor at the Day Care he had attended. She said she was tired of her job and the responsibilities. She asked me if I needed help.

I did need help. The way he was now was new to me. I had to live in his world because he could not live in mine and I didn't know what to do.

We agreed she would come in the morning, bathe and dress him and stay until noontime. I don't know what I would have done without her, but it was very expensive. Thank goodness, we had his money to pay her.

She would take John into the bathroom and I would hear all kinds of noises, but they both came out okay. It was a miracle.

I always fed him breakfast before she came so after he was dressed, they would go for a walk around our neighborhood. It was a beautiful area that looked almost like a park and there was very little traffic since there was no through traffic.

Sometimes they would sit on a park bench and they always took John's Baby Dog with them. I didn't worry because the nurse had the experience to know how to handle him if need be. He never gave her any trouble. He just loved being outside.

While they were gone, I had a chance to change the bed linens. They had to be changed every day and washed because he was now incontinent. No matter how many pads I put on the bed under him and even with his nighttime diaper, they had to be changed.

Because we had a big king size bed, I still slept with him. He couldn't get up by himself, but I wanted to be there if he tried or even if he woke up and was confused.

Actually, I just wanted to be near him. It was such a good feeling after a long day to know he was ready for the night and safe in bed.

The Baby Dog would sleep on the end of the bed on my side of the bed. Usually, I was up one time during the night, but mostly we slept good through the night.

After a few months, I had to let the nurse go. It was just too expensive and he was running out of money. Also, he was better. He had adjusted to his new home and we had a routine going. I could not take him for the walks very often, but we could sit on the upper deck and enjoy being outside. We would hold hands.

He could no longer talk to me. Now and again he would say a few words, but usually would not respond to what I asked him and there was no conversation.

There was a ceramic rose on the hall table. It was very delicate and very pretty. It had no sentimental value to me at that time.

Occasionally, John would pick it up by one of its petals and bring it to me. He would say, "For you." That was all he would say, but his eyes would sparkle and his smile said all I need to hear.

Each time, I would smile and thank him and tell him how beautiful it was. Much later I would return it to the place where he found it until one day it would catch his eye and he would bring it to me again. This is a cherished memory.

One day I was in the bedroom when he came strolling in standing very tall and walked up very close to me. He said, "I am bigger than you." "Yes, you are I said. That is why you have to take care of me and not let anyone hurt me."

That made him very proud and he walked away happy. It was good to know that even though he could not say much, he seemed to understand what I was saying. If I chose my words carefully, we would be alright.

John could no longer feed himself. We started feeding him in the hospital. I fed him every meal and offered him snacks which I had to feed him, too. Usually, he sat on a stool at the kitchen counter to eat.

One day I thought I would try to see if he wanted something bad enough, would he pick it up. He loved chocolate Oreo cookies. I put a couple on a napkin and put them in front of them. I encouraged him to eat them. He looked at them for a while, but never picked one up so I fed them to him.

My uncle was in a hospital for dementia patients. When I had the nurse to stay with John, I visited him occasionally. One day I was there at lunchtime. He was much older than John. I sat with him in the dining room as he and others ate their lunch. He was slow and very deliberate, but he ate very well by himself. Had I taken this away from John by feeding him when he should have been able to feed himself?

When I left the hospital, I was very upset with myself. I went straight to John's neurologist's office and ask if I could ask her just one question. The nurse said she would try to catch her between patients so I could ask her.

My question was if she thought that I was responsible for John not being able to feed himself and explained what I had observed with my uncle. She assured me that was not so and that all dementia patients were different depending on what part of the brain was affected. I felt better, but I was not sure. I didn't stay upset with myself because I knew I was doing the best I knew how.

One good thing that came out of my visits to see my uncle was that a met an aide there and we talked. She asked me if I needed help with John and I told her that I did. She gave me the names of some people she knew very well who had experience taking care of dementia patients. This was a wonderful because it let me go out to run errands more often feeling confident that he was in good hands.

These people were not inexpensive, but they did not cost as much as the nurse. They worked a minimum of four hours so I would plan to get everything done in the four hours they were there. This included grocery shopping, haircuts and other things that would be difficult or impossible to do if I had to take John with me.

It was also important for me to have some time for myself, because I had him the other twenty hours.

Being constantly on duty to think for and take care of John, I would get very tired and stressed. If I didn't take care of myself, I could not take care of him. That is a common statement to caregivers, but it is very true.

As time went on, John became more ill and I needed more help. I contacted Hospice and a nurse would come to our home to see him. I learned a lot from her.

Hospice also provide some sitters to help give me a break. I loved that they would come on Sunday morning so I could go to Sunday School and Church. I left lunch ready for them to feed him.

Before that, I had to pay for someone to stay with him on Sunday morning. Occasionally, my granddaughters would stay with him on Sunday morning. Being in my church on Sunday gave me the strength to go through the next week. I knew God would help me and guide me through this.

Once when he was not feeling well, the Hospice nurse said she should probably do a urine test if he would let her take the urine. He would have no part of that since she was going to insert a catheter. I guess she didn't know and I didn't know at that time about condom catheters. So now what were we going to do?

That night, I put John to bed. This meant I had to position him with his back to the bed, gently push him down into a sitting position, push his shoulders back onto the bed with his head on the pillow and then lift his feet up. He had forgotten how to lay down in the bed. I tried to make a game of it because of all of the pushing and pulling so he wouldn't mind so much.

He was lying there comfortably with his pajama top on and his night-time diaper. Then he did something I had never seen him do before. He pulled his penis out of his diaper and urinated. The urine ran into the folds of his diaper in puddles. I quickly got a paper cup from the adjourning bathroom and collected enough of the urine for a test. Another miracle? I would say it was so.

I saved the urine sample for the nurse to pick up the next day so they could do a test. He did have a urinary tract infection which causes dementia patients to be very uncomfortable, but not able to say what is wrong. The nurse returned with a prescription. One day at a time.

The Hospice team kept talking to me about letting them help me find some place for him to go while a place would still take him. I just could not agree to it. I had vowed to myself that I would never let him out of my sight and I had already let him down. He had suffered because of that.

Hospice discharged him when he became able to walk unattended. They are supposed to serve patients in their last days before they die.

In addition to his neurologist, John had also been seeing the doctor who saved his life in the hospital by sending him to intensive care. After a while, I was not able to take him to the doctor's office so we talked over the phone and I faxed him messages.

This is a message I faxed to the doctor after John became more ill and harder for me to control, "Doctor K, John has become very aggressive. The aggression started about a week ago. The first time was during a bath and immediately following. I threw my hands up when he started toward me and he grabbed my hands, squeezed and shook them. He was angry. He has repeated this several times since then."

Most of the time, I have managed to jump out of his way. Yesterday morning, he followed me so I ran out of the room and shut the door to the room he was in for a while. He is worse in the morning when he first gets up before he has his Lorazapan.

This morning he let me take his diaper off, give him some milk and a Lorazapan. I didn't try to put the diaper back on him, but I did notice that he had some BM on his hand. I got a warm washcloth and took his hand to clean it. I felt it tightening into a fist so I jumped back out of the way. I went into my room and locked the door for about 30 minutes. When I came out, he was fine. The Lorazapan had done its work and it lasts for about six hours.

I don't think he would act this way if he knew who I was. Sometimes he seems to know and sometimes he doesn't. His doctor didn't know of anything more we could try.

After a particular trying morning, I walked outside of the house locking the door behind me. I walked to the side of the house where I could look down at the creek and then I started to pray.

I didn't want to give him up. I couldn't stand the thought of him being away from me, but I wasn't managing very well.

Then a message came into my mind so very clear that I believed it was God telling me, "It is time".

I knew what I had to do for John's sake and for mine. I had to let him go where he could get the help he needed, where doctors could actually see him and the staff would know how to help him.

I turned to the Veteran's Administration for help. He met the qualifications for their help. It was not easy to get him into the hospital. There was endless paperwork and requests for medical documentation.

Finally, I contacted a local congressman and his office took over the process. After that it didn't take long for us to get a date for him to go to the VA hospital about fifty miles away.

CHAPTER 16
To The VA Hospital

The day came when it was time to take John to the VA hospital. My daughter went with us because I knew I couldn't do it by myself. John liked her a lot so this was just a fun day for him, but my heart was breaking.

I was very impressed with the hospital. It was very nice, modern and extremely well cared for. All of the people we met were pleasant and helpful.

They showed us his room. He would be sharing the room with another man. It was comfortable and had a big bathroom adjourning it equipped with all of the things necessary to take care of a person who needed help in bathing and other things.

The shower was big and open. That was good because he would not go into our master bath shower in our home. Our shower was in a small area with a door that separated the shower and toilet from the rest of the bathroom. He would get to the door and stop. For some reason he was afraid of the small space.

He had to shower in the bathroom that had a tub/shower combination and it was hard getting him into and out of the tub, but it was an open space that he did not fear.

There were many men at the hospital walking about and there was also a garden area where they could go outside. John did not have a clue what was going on so he was really enjoying all of this.

There were registered nurses on the ward and doctors readily available. All of this was really nice. There was just one thing missing. I could not stay with him.

Would he be alright? Would he be scared once he realized I was gone?

How could I do this? How could I leave him here? It was the hardest thing I had ever done. I wanted to take his hand and run out of the door, but I knew I could not.

I told him we had to leave, but we would be back. He looked confused, but not too upset. They distracted him as we left and I cried all of the way home.

I was told not to come back for a week, but I was there the next morning. I could not help it. This was the first of daily visits for months and then every other day for several years. His doctor had been wrong, he was not going to die in six months.

The seasons came and went. The highway to the hospital was four lanes so I could relax and enjoy watching some of the trees, like the redbuds, put on their Springtime dresses of bright purple and green. In the fall, the leaves of yellow and gold from the big oak trees shared the stage with the evergreens. It was quite a show.

The fifty-mile drive took about an hour from my house to the hospital, but I always looked forward to going. As I neared the hospital, I would get butterflies in my stomach with excitement. I not only loved him, I was still in love with him.

CHAPTER 17
First Visit Home

John came home with me this weekend. I wanted to bring him home so we could spend more time together. I hoped to get more insight into what he might be feeling and what he was capable of doing since he seemed to be improving. If he had not changed significantly, it wouldn't really matter. I would just enjoy being with him.

At the hospital, I initiated most of the moments of affection. He would respond to a kiss or holding my hand with loving expressions, but I would initiate most of these actions.

At home, I would be busy preparing meals, making the bed and other chores. I wanted to see if he would approach me and show affection. He did not.

A male nurse from his ward at the hospital helped me get him in the car. I told John that it was our car, mine and his and I could tell this pleased him.

John slept most of the way home. He seemed very tired and withdrawn. I knew he had been given a shower that morning and I know this can be a very frightening experience for a person with dementia. I suspected this could be the problem.

I had asked the nursing assistants at the hospital to be sure and wash his hair last. I had been advised by a professional person to do this because getting their head wet is very disturbing to a person with dementia. I hoped they were doing that.

After a struggle, I managed to get John into the house. He had forgotten how to go up steps, but I managed to help him lift his foot while he held onto the door frame. Once he got started, he was able to finish the two steps into the house.

At first, he didn't seem to know where he was. He walked around and looked at things. I tried to reassure him and make him comfortable. I sat him down in his recliner and he slept most of the afternoon with his arms folded across his chest. I worried that he might not sleep during the night, but I knew he must need the rest. One step at the time. That is all I can do.

We had his favorite dinner of chicken strips and cold slaw and he seemed to be getting more comfortable with his surroundings.

We ate in the kitchen sitting on bar stools. The stools are a little too high and not comfortable for any length of time unless you put your feet on the foot rest. I had never been able to get him to do this before, but I noticed that he was doing it that night. This was the first of small improvements that I observed.

We slept most of the night. It was so good to know that he was there beside me. Several times, I realized that he was awake, but he did not attempt to get up. He made little noises with his mouth and would laugh occasionally. I put my arms around him and talked to him. He didn't respond very much, but he didn't resist.

Saturday morning, he awoke in a great mood. He had always been this way and had carried that trait with him into his illness.

This reinforces my growing belief that although the ability of dementia patients to make responsible decisions, perform tasks as they once did and control their emotions is lost, much of their basic personality remains the same.

I invited his daughter and sister to come to see him. They and their families came and John got to see his granddaughter for the first time. He looked at her intently, but I am not sure that he fully understood. Then, again, I am not sure he didn't know what was going on.

The weekend went too fast and it was time to take him back to the hospital. I wanted so much to keep him at home with me, but I knew he needed the constant monitoring and care that he received there.

I wish our ages had been reversed and that he had been the older one and I the younger one. I would have been stronger then and I could have cared for him better. I was sixty-eight now and the days and nights of pulling him up and helping him lie down had taken its toll.

My heart ached as I helped him down the steps and to the car. I was not sure I could get him into the car, but I had to try. I worried that in the short time that it took to walk to the car he might walk away from me. What would I do? I couldn't physically stop him if he didn't want to be stopped.

I finally got him into the car like I had seen the attendant at the hospital do, but he wouldn't sit back in the seat. He was leaning back, but he was seated too far on the front of the seat. I tried to pull him up from behind, but I was not strong enough.

I started the car hoping he would sit upright on his own. Maybe instinct would take over when his back got tired, but it didn't happen.

About 10 miles down the road, I stopped at a convenience store which was just off of the interstate. We could not ride all of the way to the hospital with him sitting like that.

About the time I pulled up, two men came out of the store to get on their motorcycles which were parked beside our car. I have to take a chance, oh Lord, I have to ask them to help me.

I explained to them that he had Alzheimer Disease and what the problem was. I asked if one of them would get in the backseat of the car, reach over the front seat and put their arms under his and pull him upright. I had seen the male nurse at the hospital do this.

They looked at me in surprise, but one of them got in the back seat of the car, reached over the back and put his hands under John's arms so that he could pull him back into his seat. We were soon on our way. I was so grateful and I thanked him for his help.

A few minutes down the road, I had time to relax and thought about what I had just done. My knees were weak from freight. I didn't know who these men were. My pocketbook was in the backseat of the car. I was driving a late model Lincoln car. My actions were not those of a responsible-thinking person and I thanked God for taking care of us. Angels come in all forms and appear everywhere.

Patricia Sanderfer

What I should have done before I left our town was to go by a fire station and ask for help to get John comfortable in his seat. They would have been glad to help.

I turned the radio on loud because I knew that was the way he liked it. I wished he could talk to me. I did so want to know what he was thinking. Even though he couldn't answer me, I chatted away like I always do.

When we got back to the hospital, I opened the door and tried to help him out. I could tell by the look on his face that he didn't want to get out and he wouldn't relax enough for me to pull him around to get his feet on the ground. This was so hard, I didn't want to take him inside of the hospital and leave him again.

I had to run inside and get help. I closed the door and hoped he would not get out before I could get back. A couple of nurses came back with me and with a lot of coaching and pulling, we were able to finally get him out of the car and into the building. He wasn't so much resisting as he just wasn't cooperating. Even though he was very thin, he was almost six feet tall.

I kept telling myself that it wasn't that he didn't want to go back into the hospital. It was just that he didn't want to stop riding, but I didn't know for sure.

I stayed with him and fed him dinner. I sat by his bed and held his hand until he went to sleep. He looked so peaceful and so handsome while he slept. I kissed him gently on the forehead. We are going to be okay, my love. With God's help, we will be okay and get through this.

The days turned into weeks and we both adjusted very well. The other men on the ward were older than John. I was not uncomfortable around them at all. They seemed like children, not playful, but with a simple sweetness with a look of innocence.

I was always there to feed him at least one meal, usually lunch. So that I could see how well he was eating. Even though I wasn't eating, I felt like we were having lunch together. Some of the men could feed themselves and others needed help.

They were given a lot of food, a meat, a starch and a vegetable. He loved coco cola so that is what he usually got on his tray along with juice and always, a dessert. Occasionally, the men would eat their dessert first. Well, why not?

I had always had a very weak stomach and the smallest thing that happened at dinner time would make me feel sick. Not so in this dining room. If food was all over the mouths of the patients or dropping on their bibs, it didn't bother me at all.

I marveled at what could make this change in me. Was it because I thought of them as children?

One day during lunch, one of the men, who was seated at a round table for six, kept pushing the table forward a little bit which was annoying for the other men. I saw a nurse watching him. She asked him to stop. Next, he picked up the edge of the table a little bit so she came back and told him that if he didn't stop, he would get a court martial. He was a retired Air Force major.

I don't think she realized what a devastating affect this would have on him. He got up from the table and sat down at another table, put his head down on his arms and started to cry. I usually tried not to get involved in what was going on around us, but I couldn't stand this.

I went over to where he was, put my arm across his shoulder and told him he wasn't going to be court martialed. I even kissed him on the top of the head. He raised his head and stopped crying. He got up and walked away. I knew he would be alright because in a few hours or tomorrow, he would not remember this ever happened.

I am sure John was watching, but he was not bothered at all by my actions.

After lunch I would take John to his room and help him lay down for a nap. I sat in a chair by his bed and sometimes I dozed off, too.

When he awoke, I would let someone know and they would change his diaper. I could not do it while he was lying down because he could not help me and I was not strong enough to do it. They had a system that I never learned.

After that, we would help him stand up and he was off doing his favorite thing, walking around the very large room where most of them sat during the day. All of the patient rooms opened off of this large room and the nurse's station was there, too. He would walk this circle for hours. I bought him the best walking shoes I could find and he seemed to like them.

Patricia Sanderfer

CHAPTER 18
The Birth of John's Granddaughter

John's first and only grandchild was born today. I was sitting with John in his room at the hospital while he took his afternoon nap when his son-in-law called to say that the baby had been born. He said she was a healthy baby girl and that the baby and John's daughter were doing fine.

I thought John was asleep while I was talking to him, but when I looked at him, he had a big grin on his face and his eyes were sparkling. I said to John, "Baby", John, your grandbaby has been born and she and your daughter are doing fine." He looked at me and said, "Baby". He didn't really need to communicate with words, his expression said it all.

After I left John's hospital, I went to the Medical Center to see the baby. I wished with all of my heart that I could take him with me, but I wasn't sure whether or not I could get him in and out of the car and into the hospital safely.

During the ride, I kept thinking about how he would have loved this child. I knew he would want to teach her how to fish like he did his daughter or maybe he would just like to take her outside and teach her about nature. Long before then, he told me he didn't hunt anymore; he would rather just enjoy seeing the animals walking around.

When I got to the hospital where the baby had been born, I held the baby in my arms and rocked her. She was beautiful and looked just like her father. As I looked into her face, I thought, "I'm going to tell you all about your grandfather when you get old enough to understand. I am going to tell you how quickly he learned things and how seriously he took his responsibilities."

I pray that he stays as alert as he is now and will be able to see her and know who she is. I hope his daughter will help me find a way for him to see her.

Today when I went to the hospital to see John, the head nurse, had printed messages on two sheets of pink paper. The messages read, "John is a grandpa. It is a baby girl. She put one on his room door under his picture and one on the bottom of his glassed-in bulletin board. Where he could lay in bed and look at it.

While I was feeding him lunch, I asked him if he was glad that he had a baby girl to love. He said, "Sure" with emotion and a smile on his face. Then I started trying to get him to say her name. Finally, he said it. This was really good for him. He can answer questions sometimes with a word or two, but to follow instructions to say a word was rare.

After lunch he took a nap. I dozed in the chair beside his bed. When he awoke, he looked at me and smiled and looked around the room for a few minutes.

I noticed a piece of lint on his face, so I said to him, "Let me brush the lint from your face." As I raised my hand to brush away the lint, he took my hand and held it to his mouth. With his eyes closed, he kissed the palm of my hand and then held it to his cheek.

There were no words he could have said that would have made me feel any more loved than I did at that moment.

The baby was born in June. John's birthday was the following September so I asked the hospital if I could bring him home for the weekend. I wanted him to celebrate his birthday with his family. They approved the visit home and his family came to be with him.

He looked at his daughter holding the tiny baby, but I am not sure he fully understood that this baby was his grandchild and was the baby they had been talking to him about at the hospital. We did not offer to let him hold her and he did not try to reach for her. Sometime, it is better to be cautious.

The visit was lovely and I hoped that his daughter would bring her to the hospital when she was a little older. Children often came to the hospital and the patients loved their visits and the children loved the patients.

The nurses at the hospital had started calling John, Papa John, and they even bought a baby doll to teach him how to hold her.

John was aware that the doll was not a baby and really didn't want much to do with it. The effort to buy the doll was not wasted. There were other men on the ward who loved the baby doll. There was always someone holding the doll, rocking it and even talking to it.

Soon more dolls appeared in the ward so there would be one for everyone who wanted to hold a doll. It was so sweet to see these old men showing affection to these dolls, because they were probably fathers and grandfathers who were remembering their babies. Their minds had become childlike and children love to pretend.

This visit was the last time John saw his granddaughter until she was two or three years old. Her mother brought her to the hospital to see him.

By this time, he was in the bed permanently. For some reason, she was afraid of him. I didn't understand this because children were in and out of the hospital all of the time and they seemed to love the old "grandfathers".

Even though he wasn't able to talk by then, except to occasionally make a sound, the children who were visiting another patient would talk to John and some of them would even try to climb up on his bed.

This was sad for me, because I knew how much he loved children and how much he would have loved his granddaughter if he had been given the chance to have a normal life.

Before she was born, I knew his daughter was trying to have a baby and had been for a long time. I prayed and prayed that God would give them a baby and that the baby would come while John was still alive.

Most days were uneventful and calm. One of my sweetest memories was when one of the men walked up to me with his hands cupped together in front of him like he was holding something.

He held his empty hands in front of me and said, "these are for you."
I asked, "What are they?"
He said, "blueberries". I held my hands out and he went through the

motions like he was pouring them into my hands. I thanked him and he asked what I was going to do with them.

I said, "I will make a delicious Blueberry pie." His face was radiant as he walked away.

Sometimes the patients didn't understand what they were seeing. On day I entered the ward to find a patient sitting in a big comfortable chair.

He wasn't a tall man, but he was a little chubby and had an adorable personality. He had his little legs pulled up under him in the chair and he looked concerned.

I asked, "How are you,"

He said, "There is water everywhere." The floor was very shiny because it had just been polished.

I said, "No, there is no water, the floor is just shining because it is so clean." Then I stood in front of him and moved my feet on the floor. He smiled and I wished him a good morning.

Later, I saw him walking around.

CHAPTER 19
Quarterly Meeting

Today, I went to the VA hospital for John's quarterly evaluation. During the evaluation, members of the team responsible for his well-being were present. Among them was the head nurse, the physician's assistant, the recreational therapist, pharmacist, psychiatrist, social worker, and others. I was excited about this visit because John was doing so well. I had the option of taking John with me or attending the meeting alone. I usually opted to attend the meeting alone, because I was not sure what he understood and what he didn't. I didn't want him hear negative things that might affect him.

John went with me on this day, because it was a happy day. I walked into the room and said, "this is show and tell. I brought John with me today so you could see what a good job you are doing."

The nurse in charge of his ward, added her good words about his increased ability to communicate, that he was noticing more things, picking things up and had a more relaxed demeanor.

I was feeling as pleased as punch until another person spoke up. She said, that with these newly found abilities, John was exhibiting "inappropriate sexual behavior." I was shocked. For the last three years, John had shown no awareness or interest in sex.

I asked her what she meant. She very dramatically explained, while glancing around the room at the almost totally male attendees, that he had touched the breast of a patient's daughter.

Also, he was alleged to have said, "I want to f—k.", in front of a health-care aide. Inappropriate behavior on a dementia ward? The men were the patients and other people were supposed to be trained to respond appropriately.

I could hardly believe my ears. While I was with John, I hugged him, kissed him, rubbed his back, held his hand.

He kissed me back, hugged me and held my hand to his mouth and kissed my hand, but he never touched me in a sexual way.

I didn't touch him that way either, because I thought he might not understand and be offended.

During this time, there was a lot of laughter. I sort of laughed along, but my heart felt sick. I felt I should somehow defend his actions.

I told them that he never touched me in that way and that I knew he hugged people, but that the people who told me that he hugged them seemed to be happy about it.

I asked how they thought he would be able to tell who wanted to be hugged and who would not. He can't even ask for a drink of water. It would amaze me if he could express a desire to have sex.

The team seemed to have a great time with a story of how he had hugged a particularly strait-laced, prim lady during their morning walks through the hospital. She was a member of the hospital staff and I got the impression she was not very well-liked.

The recreational therapist, who worked on John's ward, took the men, who are able to walk well enough, on walks down the hall of the hospital so they could experience a different environment for a while. It is also a great way for them to get exercise.

Maybe John thought he knew the lady or maybe he just thought she looked like she needed a hug. Whatever he thought, John went up to her and gave her a hug. The people on the medical team who were hearing this story for the first time thought it was hilarious. They said they wished they had a picture of John hugging this woman.

John did not laugh. Maybe he didn't know they were talking about him. After a few minutes, he stood up and the meeting was over. Before I left the room, they assured me that they were not going to change his medication.

Later, I talked to the nurse administrator of the ward. I told her that I understood them having fun with his behavior, but for a family member, it is not funny.

I said, "This is my best friend, the love of my life, my husband and I don't want his actions to be laughed at. It was humiliating for me." She said she understood. I hoped this would help other family members who were put in that position.

CHAPTER 20
Fateful Day

Then the fateful day came. At a monthly meeting, they told me that John was going to be moved to another ward. This was an all-bed ward. I begged them not to move him and put him in a bed. They said he had been falling a lot.

They had done some additional tests on him and were sure his condition was not going to improve. They even changed some of his medication, but he didn't improve. He was not causing problems.

I felt like they wanted to get rid of me because I was there so much of the time.

On one occasion and another, I had become known by people in other parts of the hospital, even the director. Maybe this was the reason, but I did not know. No one had indicated that I was there too much.

If they stopped him from walking, I knew it was going to be the beginning of the end.

Patricia Sanderfer

CHAPTER 21
New Ward

The new ward was very nice and there was even more staff on duty. The doctors made rounds pretty often and there was always one or more registered nurses on duty. He shared the room with another patient like before except this patient was in a bed, too.

In the beginning, a physical therapist would come to his bed, but that soon stopped because he could not follow her directions to lift a foot or whatever she needed him to do.

It broke my heart to see him lying there. He was so very thin and I knew he would lose muscles if he did not use them.

His roommates seldom had visitors so I would try to cheer them up a little, too. Sometimes, they would decide to die. They would just stop eating and no amount of coaching from me or the nurses would get them to eat.

Sometimes, I would ask them if I could feed them and they would smile and say, "No, thank you."

Most of them could talk and they would thank whomever was talking to them and just say they were not hungry. They would not drink anything either.

Outside of the room, I talked to the nurses. They said this was not uncommon and they could not force anyone to eat or drink. It was against the rules. I asked how long it would be before they died and they said approximately 20 days because they already had health issues.

The last one I saw do this had been John's roommate for a long time. I realized that he had stopped eating. I asked if he had any family and they said the family had been notified. She said the families always come about the time the patient was going to die.

One day, when I came in, John's roommate had died. His bed was empty and they were sanitizing his room getting it ready for the next patient. I guess I missed the family, but I didn't ask. I didn't want to know.

They had put John in his chair and moved him into the atrium while they prepared the room. He must have known about the death, but we could not talk about it. Hopefully, in a day or two, he would not remember if it had upset him. I just gave him a hug and a kiss on the forehead and tried to be cheerful.

Every visit, I would hold his hand and tell him how much I loved him. He never removed his hand from mine and he held it firmly. When it was time to go, I would kiss his hand and remove mine. When he was able, before he got really sick, he would kiss my hand often.

Patricia Sanderfer

CHAPTER 22
The Dentist

I tried to brush John's teeth after he ate, but he hated that. He would make a hurt face and try to pull away. I wondered if his teeth had once again become decayed or if he just didn't like something hard being put in his mouth. I tried a very soft tooth brush and even an electric toothbrush, but nothing worked.

I looked in his mouth, the best I could, and his teeth did not look good. I asked the nurses if they would schedule an examination with the dentist. There were dentists who worked in an area of the hospital.

Finally, his appointment came and they took him up to the dentist offices on another floor. My worst concerns were true. He needed dental work, but they were not equipped to put dementia patients to sleep and he could not cooperate with them like he did the first time we had his dental work done when his illness had not progressed so far.

This was not acceptable. I had to do something.

I went up to the dentist offices of the hospital and talked to the dentist in charge. He explained the situation to me. He said that they were very disappointed that they didn't have the equipment, because there were many patients in the hospital that needed to be put to sleep before a dental procedure could be done.

Also. they needed the equipment for some of the veterans who came there as outpatients. Many attempts had been made to make the equipment available to the dentist offices.

I finally got permission for John to be treated on a contract basis with a private dentist nearby. The hospital chose a dentist who had an office near the hospital and his main office was in the town where I lived. He said he could only do this extensive procedure in his main office.

Once a patient is admitted to a VA hospital, they, not the family, have total control of their treatment.

I was told that I should go to the office of the dentist who was going to do John's dental work before the procedures were scheduled to be done. I needed to sign papers giving them permission to do whatever was necessary.

I understood that if he was put to sleep, he might not wake up again. This was not a hard decision, because I knew that living with a toothache was not an option. I talked to his daughter and she agreed. We had to take the chance.

I went to the dentist office to sign the papers for the dental work to be done. There were many papers, but I knew they were to protect the dentist if anything went wrong. I understood that after glancing at the first couple of pages and then I started signing anywhere there was an "X" without reading all of the fine details.

I would not normally sign something I had not read and the words of a previous employer, a judge, went through my mind. When I worked for him, I sometimes signed a contract and then brought it in for him to look at. I guess I was just wanting affirmation that I had done the right thing. One day he told me not to ever sign anything until I was sure it was the right thing to do. So, I said out loud, I am glad Judge Phillips can't see me signing these papers without reading them.

The lady who brought me the papers asked how I knew Judge Phillips. I explained that I had worked for him as the Court Reporter of State Court and added how much I had respected and admired him. We were still friends in that I could call him if I wanted his opinion and occasionally stopped by his office in the courthouse to say hello.

She told me that the dentist and Judge Phillips were very close friends.

The lady left for a few minutes and when she came back, she said the dentist wanted to know if I could stay until he finished what he was doing so that he could talk to me. I told her that I would love to talk to him.

Soon the dentist came out and we went into one of the small counseling rooms where we could talk. He wanted to know what the situation was at the hospital that they couldn't do the dental work needed.

I told him about visiting with the dentists at the hospital and what they told me about not having the necessary equipment to put a patient to sleep if that was necessary. They not only saw patients at the hospital, but veterans in the area who qualified for their help.

The dentist asked me when I would be at the hospital during the next week. He wanted to examine John there and he wanted me to go with him to talk to the dentists who worked at the hospital.

I told him I could be there any day that was convenient for him. He told me to come to his office that was near the hospital on Tuesday of the next week and we would go to the hospital together after he had seen his patients that day.

I was happy to do what the dentist asked. I went to his office and waited until he had finished with his patients. I drove my car to the hospital. The dentist met me there.

When we entered John's room, I explained to John who the dentist was and that he wanted to examine his teeth.

I don't know if he understood what I was telling him, but thankfully he cooperated as the dentist used a flash light to look inside of his mouth. The dentist could not hide his concern about the condition of John's teeth.

After the examination was over, we went to another floor of the hospital where we had an appointment to talk to the dentists there. The dentist in charge of the dentist office at the hospital seemed very pleased that there was someone he could talk to about the lack of the proper equipment. His efforts through the regular channels of the hospital had not produced any results.

I listened as they talked for a while. About the only thing they said to me was that I should know that John might not wake up after being put to sleep. I told them that I did understand that, but he could not be allowed to suffer from bad teeth and a tooth ache that he could not even tell me about.

In a few days, I met the ambulance that had brought John to the dentist's main office in the town where I lived. I would not have been able to make the trip with him. He was on a stretcher and appeared to be asleep. When he woke up, I stood by the stretcher and talked to him and held his hand. He seemed very calm.

I waited in the waiting room and prayed for what seemed like forever while the dentist completed his work. I could not allow myself to think that he could not wake up. He had to wake up and his mouth heal.

The procedure was finally over. A lot of work had been done. Teeth that could not be repaired were pulled and others filled. We stayed there until he was awake and they were sure he was alright. Then he was put him back into the ambulance and taken him back to the hospital. I was assured that he was not in pain.

I thanked the dentist and his staff and I thanked God for letting me have my John for a little longer.

I never knew the details of what happened later. I don't know if the dentist and the judge had anything to do with it, but the hospital dental office got the equipment they needed to take care of their patients. This was a blessing for so many patients.

One thing I do know. God works in mysterious ways and uses anyone that is available to do his will.

So why does God let people get hurt or sick to start with? Everyone has their own opinions about this, but mine is that we were not promised a perfect world on this earth so he just lets things happen naturally. If we believe and pray, he will answer our prayers in his own way and in his own time. Someone else may have a better answer.

Days, weeks and months went by. Some were notable, but most were about the same. John did not improve and he was a little more than a skeleton with skin stretched over it.

He was as comfortable as they could make him. His hospital bed pulsated every minute or two to help with circulation and help to keep him from having bed sores. He was turned several times a day because he could not turn himself.

Several days a week they put John and the other patients in their geri chairs. John's geri chair was blue. It was softly padded and could be adjusted to many levels. He could sit up to eat his meals and then lay back where he could comfortably nap if he wanted to.

Patients like John, who could not help at all with getting into their chairs, were put into the chairs with a motorized lift.

The lift was like a sling or hammock. The nurses would put a canvass under him that had hooks on it and this machine would lift him out of the bed into his chair.

It was things like this that reassured me that this hospital was where he needed to be.

The chairs were rolled into an atrium that was glass enclosed and the patients could see outside. This was also a room where they could eat at large round tables.

Occasionally, groups of people came to the hospital to entertain the patients with songs. There was a piano in the atrium. The atrium was cheerfully decorated and there were flowers in the middle of each table.

Members of the military from the Air Force base that was nearby came and talked to the patients that were able to talk with them. They were in uniform and the men really liked that since they were all veterans.

Sometimes the visitors would stop at John's chair if he was in the atrium or come to his bed if he was in his room. He could not talk to them, but I would tell them about his Air Force career and they would thank him for his service. From the expression on his face I could see that he was proud.

One of the best things about the atrium was that the patients could see each other and people coming in and out of the hospital. We humans, need social contact with each other.

The hospital aids put boots on John's feet so he would not get sores on his heels due to contact with the bed.

He was kept clean and his body was rubbed with lotions to protect his skin.

By now, his food had to be pureed, because if he could chew, he would probably not do it very well. There was always a lot of fruit and fruit juice on the trays and usually a dessert and a cup of ice cream.

There was also a can of a nutritional drink on his tray. I would take the drink and mix it with his ice cream to make a milkshake. He especially liked the milkshake and he could drink out of a straw.

Most days he would eat pretty well. I enjoyed feeding him.

CHAPTER 23
Good Bye, My Love

Lately, he had not been eating much at all. His ability to swallow even the pureed food and thickened liquids was getting worse. He was so terribly thin that I hated to raise the sheet and see what was left of his body. I feared the worse.

One day, I walked into the room and John was asleep. That was not unusual so I just sat down beside his bed. He looked so peaceful, the curls of his dark hair sprinkled with gray against the white of the pillow was beautiful.

I marveled that his skin was so pretty even though he was sixty-four years old. His face was thin like the rest of his body, but a good diet and the creams the nurses put on his body was a tribute to the care he received.

I gently called his name, but there was no response. I went about my normal habit of checking to see if everything was alright.

I looked to see if his diaper was clean and how his skin was doing in that area.

I adjusted the pillow that someone had put between his knees. He was laying on his side and one thin knee would press on the other. He seemed to be alright.

Maybe if I let him continue to sleep, he could stay awake better when the food tray came, I thought.

I sat down close to his bed and held his hand in mine. This time he did not grasp my hand back.

Every time I took his hand, I was reminded how much he loved to hold hands. I loved it, too, and would say to myself that I would always remember how it felt to hold his hand.

After a while, I could hear the rumble of the food trays coming down the hall and the good smell of the food.

It was remarkable how good they could make the food taste even though it was pureed. They told me that the pureed food was the same food that they served to the men who could chew and swallow without choking.

The food service attendant came in with the usual cheery hello and placed his tray on the table that they would normally slide in front of him.

Since he could not feed himself, I put the table to the side of his bed and sat facing him so he could look at me.

I often told him how much fun it was to have dinner with him. Of course, I never ate from his tray. Sometimes I would taste the food to know what I was feeding him.

I don't suppose he knew that. I never knew what he knew or didn't know.

Today was no exception. He had a meat, two vegetables, fruit, thickened beverage and dessert. Because I had told the dietitian a long time ago how much he loved ice cream, there was always a small cup of ice cream on his tray in addition to everything else.

The menu was one he seemed to favor so I hoped he would eat good today. I said, "John, wake up", but he didn't respond.

I started turning him into position on his back where I could feed him. He opened his eyes briefly as I positioned him in the bed, but then closed them again.

"Wake up, John, we need to eat dinner," I said. I got a warm wash cloth and washed his face gently.

He looked at me briefly and went back to sleep. The food was always very hot so I thought I would let him sleep a few minutes more. Maybe he was up in his chair today and was more tired than usual.

"John, wake up sweetheart, we need to eat.' I said. They will come for your tray soon and you will be hungry tonight."

I started taking things off of his tray that I could keep for later if he would not wake up now.

I emptied his water glass and filled it with his canned drink, added his ice cream and a thickener. I stirred it until it became a milk shake.

If he could not wake up enough to eat now, he could at least drink the milkshake later. He would always drink his milkshake, I thought, so I didn't start to worry right away.

John's roommate's wife, had come in earlier to feed her husband.

We were so lucky to share a room with them. His roommate had been a surveyor before he retired. He was a kind, gentle man who never gave anyone any trouble.

Even though he was diabetic and had to have his blood sugar checked several times a day and sometime received a shot, he never complained.

His wife was the impediment of southern charm and grace. She was always dressed immaculately with every hair of her auburn hair in place. Her biggest asset was her sweet smile and charming ways.

She lived less than a mile from the hospital so, even though she was a few years older than me, she was there almost every day. It made us both feel good that there was someone besides the staff in the room for a lot of the time.

The staff was in and out of the rooms all day and night, but they had many patients to care for so their time in one room was limited.

After John's roommate had finished eating, his wife asked me how John was doing.

"Not well," I said. He opens his eyes about every five minutes like he is startled, but he goes back to sleep before I can get him to drink very much. If I put food in his mouth, it just stays on the tip of his tongue until I remove it.

He was shaking badly when he woke up. "Can you see him from over there?" I asked.

"Yes," she said, "it looks like he is very cold." The room was warm and he felt warm so I was confused. I pulled his bed spread a little closer over his shoulders, but he did not stop shaking.

A nurse came into the room to see how well the men had eaten.

"There is something wrong with John," I said. I explained to her what had been happening.

John sleeping or not eating was not too uncommon so she was not overly concerned, but she said she would make a note of it and have someone check him out.

He didn't have a fever or any other signs of a medical problem different from what we already knew. We concluded that he was very tired.

There was no explanation for the shaking. Through the years, he had gone through many different experiences. I put a little extra cover on him.

Eventually, I went home after getting the staff to promise me that they would keep trying to get him to drink something and let me know if anything changed.

I kept telling myself that after sleeping through the night, he would be better in the morning. I thanked God that, except for the shaking when he woke up, he didn't seem to be suffering.

The next morning, I called the hospital after they had a chance to make their morning rounds to get an update on the patients and asked how John was.

They had put him in his geri chair and put him in the atrium hoping this would stimulate his mind to stay awake, but he had not eaten breakfast and stayed the same.

By the time I got to the hospital, they had put him back in his bed. I took his hand and his fingers closed over mine. His eyes were still closed and he looked so peaceful.

"Is this the way he is going to go?" I asked our Lord. This is a good way; just to go to sleep peacefully and not wake up, but the choice was not mine to make so we would just take one day at a time.

I am not going to let myself start to grieve, I told myself. We had been through so many times when we thought he was not going to make it and, somehow, he had miraculously pulled through.

What I needed to do was to get someone's attention to make sure they were not missing something that was going on with him beyond the normal symptoms of his disease.

I talked to everyone who came into the room on the hospital staff telling them that something was not right. His episodes of waking up were about five minutes apart. He would wake up with a startled look on his face, start shaking and then go back to sleep.

I took this precious minute to talk to him and try to get a few sips of thickened liquid in his mouth. Sometimes he would swallow and sometimes it would run back out of his mouth onto the towel that was spread across his chest.

Later in the day, the doctor came into the room and examined John. Still no fever or signs of discomfort beyond the shaking.

Since people were seldom there during the brief moments that he was shaking, it was hard to explain. The doctor said she would have some tests run.

The tests came back negative except for a slight kidney infection. The doctor ordered an antibiotic and the days went on without much change. The shaking was not as pronounced and he woke up less.

My John, my dear John, please wake up and eat something. I kept talking to him and telling him how much I loved him and how much God loved him.

I also talked to him about the weather and what was going on around us or anything else I could think of to say.

When the nurses came in to change his diaper or roll him over, they would talk to him, too, but there was no response in his expression.

On the morning of the fourth day, my daughter called as she did every day to see how he was. "I guess I need to call his sister and his daughter," I said to my daughter. "I don't know if they want to be bothered since he doesn't have any trauma going on."

She said she thought I should call them. "You do the right thing, Mama. At least they will know how he is," she said.

I couldn't reach his daughter, but was able to talk to his sister at work. She said she would get in touch with his daughter for me.

After a while, the daughter called me. I went over his test results and his symptoms. Since she was a registered nurse, I presumed she was trying to make a determination. "That just doesn't make any sense," she said.

I said, "Since you are off from work today, why don't you go to see your Dad?" "Oh, I plan to go," she said. "I will be leaving in a little bit."

Since she would be with him, I decided to stay at home and get some rest. It was not the trip down there that was so hard, it was the worry and the stress that wore me out.

About 10:30 his daughter called. She said she didn't see anything wrong with him. She said he was sitting in the atrium sleeping peacefully and that every now and then he would open his eyes and then go back to sleep.

I asked if he was still shaking when he woke up. She said she hadn't noticed, but there was some kind of celebration going on in the atrium and she had been watching that.

The tone of her voice sounded to me like she was totally outdone that I had caused her to take her day off from work to drive down there when there was nothing wrong with him. I asked her if she would please stay and feed him lunch and she said she would.

My heart was so heavy and this was the straw that broke the camel's back. Why did I call her? She had not been to see him more than a couple of times in the last year; not on his birthday or any of the holidays. Why did I think she would want to go now?

How did I know she had not been there? I knew because when anyone came to see John, everyone on the staff who saw them would tell me. Guests had to go by the Nurse's Station to get to the rooms. They see everything that goes on with their patients and they love to tell me if something good happens with John.

The tears I had been holding back started and just wouldn't stop. I loved John so much. I didn't know what he knew. He was a good father and loved his daughter and his family so much.

Soon after lunch, I got another call from his daughter. This time she was tearful. She said, "He is gone, I am sure of it. I tried and tried to wake him up so I could feed him, but he did nothing the whole time I was there. One of the nurses came over and tried to help me, but he would not respond."

I tried to comfort her. One part of me was glad she had seen how he was and that I had not exaggerated his condition, but I was more concerned that she was hurting and he was not responding.

I knew his daughter loved him. How could she not? She even had her own hunting clothes when she was growing up so she could go into the woods with him. He had taught her about nature and the beauty of the outdoors.

One Christmas, she had gone to his house and made him an adorable Christmas tree with woodland decorations. He was so proud of that tree because she had made it for him. Every time we talked through the years, he would tell me how proud he was of her and he always gave me pictures of her.

I wish family members of the other veterans and of sick people everywhere would realize how important it is that they be shown love.

It doesn't matter that the patient might not remember the visit. For the time that the visit is happening, they are enjoying the visit. When they are happy, good things are happening in the body that have lasting benefits.

Today was an okay day. I decided it was a good day as any to clean out the floor of my walk-in closet. As good a day as any, because no day is a good day for that chore.

I looked at John's clothes hanging there in his area of the closet. I know I should give them to someone who could use them, but it was nice to see them still hanging there.

I don't have to think about that today, I thought. I will just clean out the floor of the closet. How does it fill up so quickly with things that don't seem to belong any other place?

Then I saw his shoes. I had bought him the best walking shoes I could find when he could still walk, but these were dress shoes. Of all of the things we bought when he was still living at home, he loved those shoes the most.

I had noticed him looking at them before he put them on and admiring them on his feet. I thought they looked great on him. He wore a size 10 which is not very big for a man who was 5'11" tall. He had a pretty, slender foot.

He was self-conscious about his feet. He said he had been teased about them when he was growing up. I could not understand why. He had very nice feet.

The shoes were brown leather loafers with tassels on the front. I held them in my hands and looked at the scuff marks on the toes made after he had difficulty stepping up when he was walking. I held them in my hands for a minute and then to my chest as the tears flooded down my cheeks.

The shoes brought back memories of the first pair we bought. When he was in the other hospital, he had forced his swollen feet into the shoes until they were stretched out of shape.

As soon as I could get to a store after we came home from the hospital where he had ruined his first pair, I bought him another pair of shoes just like the first. I was thinking that I would make sure these were on his feet when he was buried. My love, my love, I miss you so.

The next day, I went back to the Veterans hospital and still there was no change with John except he had started hiccupping. In between the hiccups, I tried to give him a little liquid being careful that he did not strangle, but the hiccups did not stop.

I asked the staff if they would have the doctor come by to see him and see if there was anything she could do. The doctor had already been notified and knew what was going on. She had given him some medication to see if he could relax, but it didn't seem to be helping. Later in the day, the doctor came back into his room and told me she would keep trying.

We tried everything. We tried different positions in the bed, on his right side, on the other side, on his back. We lowered the head of bed until it was flat and raised it as high as we could without him toppling over, but nothing seemed to matter.

I was amazed and saddened to see that even when he was asleep, the hiccups didn't stop. One after the other, they never stopped. I was frantic.

I talked to him, telling him stories of his life that he knew. I talked about his grandparents that he adored who had long since passed away. I reminded him that we still had their rifles, his grandfather's and his grandmother's hunting rifles.

Still, there was no response and the hiccups went on day and night for almost a week. I could only imagine how sore his ribs must be.

One morning when I arrived at the hospital, the hiccups had stopped. I was so happy until I realized that he appeared to be very sick.

They told me that he had pneumonia. I knew this was how so many dementia patients died and so many emotions flooded though my mind.

He was soon to be released from this body that was causing him so much pain. I felt this.

How could I live without him? Each thought tugged at my heart and I decided it was selfish of me to want him to live. I prayed the prayer that I had prayed so long, "Not my will, but thine be done, oh Lord".

When the doctor came into his room to talk to me, she gave me the option of starting him on a feeding tube and moving him to intensive care.

She said they were not supposed to try to prolong the life of the patients if there was no chance of recovery, but she would do this if I wanted her to. I told her I needed to talk to his daughter and she agreed.

I talked to his daughter and we agreed that the kindest thing would be to let nature take its course, let him go to be with God and end his long battle filled with so much suffering. His body was almost a skeleton and he had nothing left to fight with.

The hospital staff moved John into a private room and started an IV. I don't know what was in the IV, but I hoped it was something to ease his pain if he was in pain. They also put an oxygen mask on his face which replaced the oxygen tubes that he previously had.

I could tell he didn't like the mask from his grimaces, but he could not remove it. The nurses told me that they were required to put the mask on him. It kept slipping up closer to his eyes and I was afraid the oxygen would burn his eyes. I kept pulling it down over his nose where it belonged. His breathing was very loud and labored.

His eyes were open now and they never closed again, but I did not know if he was conscious. His fingers still closed over mine when I held his hand like always, but was that a reflex?

I talked to him and told him how much I loved him and how much God loved him. I told him that I would not leave him and so it was for the next four days.

The hospital staff was so kind. They brought towels so I could shower in his private bathroom, but I never did.

Sometimes I would wash my face and brush my teeth and then go back to him.

Each time there was a change of staff, which was about every eight hours, many of them would come into the room to see him. They would talk to him and kiss him on the forehead as they left. His eyes were open, but he never really looked at anyone, not even me.

The staff continued to bring his tray of food three times a day, but it was no longer pureed food, it was whatever the other patients were eating. They encouraged me to eat it, because I would not leave his bedside. This was so kind of them.

One evening his family came to visit. They all came at once. They talked to John and, of course he did not respond, but his eyes were open. They laughed and talked to each other enjoying their time together. He would have enjoyed that so much.

I wish they had come together like that while he could have still enjoyed them. Christmas, Thanksgiving or maybe on his birthday would have been so nice.

This is a common mistake with families. They think that their loved one would not know they were there and not would not remember the visit so why bother.

The truth is that we don't know what dementia patients know and even if they did not remember, they would benefit from the moment of happiness.

Soon, they all left. His daughter asked me to call her if there was any change and I asked if she wanted me to call even if it was in the middle of the night. She said she wanted to know immediately.

Sometimes during the night, I would doze off sitting in the chair by his bed holding his hand. On the fourth night, I had dozed off for a few minutes and then I woke up. It was about three o'clock in the morning. I realized the heavy breathing had stopped and he was no longer holding my hand tightly.

His hand was still soft and warm. His eyes were still open, like always, but I could not tell if he was breathing. About that time a nurse came around the curtain. She attended to him and then she looked at me.

"Is he gone?", I asked.

"Yes", she said and gently closed his eyes. She said that she would leave us alone for a few minutes so I could tell him goodbye.

I had been telling him goodbye for the last eleven years and now he had left me. Now he was at peace with his God in heaven and I was at peace knowing he was not suffering.

I did the necessary things at the hospital, signing the papers in the hospital office, and letting the hospital load up my car with his belonging. I did these things like I was in a daze, my eyes were blurred with tears, but I did what had to be done.

When I left the hospital to drive back to my home which was 50 miles away, I chose to leave by driving by the lake on the back side of the hospital. The big ducks that sometimes blocked the road had all gone to roost even though the night seemed unusually bright.

I turned the corner in the road where there were no large trees blocking my view and saw the most incredibly huge moon I had ever seen in my life. It was golden in color and so large it seemed to almost touch the earth.

It was the night of March 20, 2011. Later, I would learn that it was a Parthenon Moon which was really a large full moon reaching its exact full phase within an hour of lunar perigee, the point in the moon's elliptical orbit closest to the earth.

To me, it was just a thing of beauty that gave the earth an ethereal glow.

I stopped the car and got out to better see the moon. In my mind, I could see John walking, running and dancing his way toward heaven in the light of the moon. Free at last, he was free at last from the terrible illness that had held him captive for so long.

"Go, John, Go," I cried, wishing I could go with him. "We will be together again and the next time will be forever."

ABOUT THE AUTHOR

Patricia Sanderfer loved and lived with her husband for eleven years while he battled early onset dementia. She hopes that by sharing her story that on the same journey will find comfort. Patricia currently resides in Macon, Georgia. This is her first book.

Printed in the United States
By Bookmasters